Towards Perfect Health

D1232438

Selections from the writings of the Mother and Sri Aurobindo

SRI AUROBINDO ASHRAM
PONDICHERRY

First edition 2006
Second impression 2008

(Typeset in 10.5/13 Palatino)

Cover: Painting by Krishnalal Bhatt
Title of the Painting: Unity of Consciousness

Rs 75
ISBN 978-81-7058-840-5

Published by Sri Aurobindo Ashram Publication Department
Pondicherry 605 002
Web: http://www.sabda.in

Printed at Sri Aurobindo Ashram Press, Pondicherry
PRINTED IN INDIA

Foreword

This compilation of the words of Sri Aurobindo and the Mother was first conceptualised as an Exhibition.

It is being presented here as a book because many who visited the exhibition felt that a handy volume would be a help in their life and sadhana.

The selections have been taken from the Centenary edition of the Collected works of the Mother and the Sri Aurobindo Birth Centenary Library edition.

The chapter headings, the titles for the quotations as well as a few linking sentences (in italics in the book) have been given by the compilers.

CONTENTS

CONTENTS

Introduction

Our aim

A divine perfection of the human being is our aim.

Sri Aurobindo, 21: 590

Man — a living laboratory

The animal is a living laboratory in which Nature has, it is said, worked out man. Man himself may well be a thinking and living laboratory in whom and with whose conscious co-operation she wills to work out the superman, the god.

Sri Aurobindo, 18: 4

Limitations of the human body

Still the inconveniences of the animal body and its animal nature and impulses and the limitations of the human body at its best are there in the beginning and

persist always so long as there is not the full and funda-
mental liberation and its inconscience or half-conscience
and its binding of the soul and mind and life-force to
Matter, to materiality of all kinds, to the call of the
unregenerated earth-nature are there and constantly
oppose the call of the spirit and circumscribe the climb
to higher things. To the physical being it brings a bondage to the material instruments, to the brain and heart
and senses, wed to materiality and materialism of all
kinds, to the bodily mechanism and its needs and obli-
gations, to the imperative need of food and the preoccupation with the means of getting it and storing it as
one of the besetting interests of life, to fatigue and sleep,
to the satisfaction of bodily desire.

Sri Aurobindo, 16: 25

Breaking of our limitations

The most we can do in the physical field by physical
means is necessarily insecure as well as bound by limits; even what seems a perfect health and strength of
the body is precarious and can be broken down at any
moment by fluctuations from within or by a strong attack or shock from outside: only by the breaking of our
limitations can a higher and more enduring perfection
come.

Sri Aurobindo, 16: 13

The stable basis

To discover the eternal Sachchidananda, this essential self of our being within us, and live in it is the stable basis, to make its true nature evident and creative of a divine way of living in our instruments, supermind, mind, life and body, the active principle of a spiritual perfection.

Sri Aurobindo, 21: 598

Spiritual Ananda

A spiritual Ananda can flow into the body and mundane cell and tissue; a luminous materialisation of this higher Ananda could of itself bring about a total transformation of the deficient or adverse sensibilities of physical Nature.

Sri Aurobindo, 19: 989

This human hour

This human hour, this earthly hour is beautiful over all other hours. Let each and all know it and rejoice in the plenitude that is given.

The Mother, 1: 165

The Adventure

Awakening of consciousness

The greater and greater awakening of consciousness and its climb to a higher and higher level and a wider extent of its vision and action is the condition of our progress towards that supreme and total perfection which is the aim of our existence. It is the condition also of the total perfection of the body.

Sri Aurobindo, 16: 15

Total transformation

If a total transformation of the being is our aim, a transformation of the body must be an indispensable part of it; without that no full divine life on earth is possible.

Sri Aurobindo, 16: 24

Physical consciousness

A development of the physical consciousness must always be a considerable part of our aim, but for that the right development of the body itself is an essential element; health, strength, fitness are the first needs, but the physical frame itself must be the best possible.

Sri Aurobindo, 16: 5

Be open

As we rise we have to open to them [*higher levels of the mind*] our lower members and fill these with those superior and supreme dynamisms of light and power; the body we have to make a more and more and even entirely conscious frame and instrument, a conscious sign and seal and power of the spirit.

Sri Aurobindo, 16: 15

The connection of the divine life with the life of earth

...it might be urged that the organic structure of the body no less than its basic outer form would have to be retained as a necessary material foundation for the retention of the earth-nature, the connection of the divine life with the life of earth and a continuance of the evolutionary process so as to prevent a breaking upward out of and away from it into a state of being which would properly belong to a higher plane and not to a terrestrial divine fulfilment.

Sri Aurobindo, 16: 36

Discipline

One must already be something of a sage to be able to undergo a rigorous discipline of the body and obtain from it the ordered, regular effort which can perfect it. There is no longer any room there for all the fancies of desire. You see, as soon as one gives way to excesses, to immoderation of any kind and a disorderly life, it becomes quite impossible to control one's body and develop it normally, not to mention that, naturally, one spoils one's health and as a result the most important part of the ideal of a perfect body disappears; for with bad health, impaired health, one is not much good for anything. And it is certainly the satisfaction of desires and impulses of the vital or the unreasonable demands of certain ambitions which make the body suffer and fall ill.

The Mother, 9: 99

State of consciousness

Here, it is very easy if we know one thing, that the method we use to deal with our body, maintain it, keep it fit, improve it and keep it in good health, depends *exclusively* on the state of consciousness we are in; for our body is an instrument of our consciousness and this consciousness can act directly on it and obtain what it wants from it.

The Mother, 9: 108

Not to reject the physical

Mother,

Can you tell me why in Sri Aurobindo's Ashram, in your presence, everyone seems to think of food, physical culture and the doctor for keeping good health? The Divine help may take a fourth place if it likes. It is difficult, at present, for one to speak of your help. People seem to think that by speaking of your help either one is trying to show off or is a fanatic.

Sri Aurobindo said that the physical was to be taken into the yoga and not rejected or neglected. And almost all here thought they were doing yoga in the physical and fell the prey of the physical "needs" and desires...

To speak frankly, I like better that mistake than that of the so-called ascetics who are full of contempt, bad will and scornful feelings for the others.

The Mother, 17: 306

In the physical consciousness

So, for all those who live on the physical plane, in the physical consciousness, it is physical means and processes which have to be used in dealing with the body. And as the vast majority of human beings, even in the Ashram, live in a consciousness which, if not exclusively physical is at least predominantly physical, it is quite natural for them to follow and obey all the principles laid down by physical science for the care of the body.

The Mother, 9: 109

Be perfect

To understand the true reason why you are here, you must remember that we want to become instruments that are as perfect as possible, instruments that express the divine will in the world. And if the instruments are to be perfect, they must be cultivated, educated, trained. They must not be left like fallow land or a formless piece of stone. A diamond reveals all its beauty only when it is artistically cut. It is the same for you. If you want your physical being to be a perfect instrument for the manifestation of the supramental consciousness, you must cultivate it, sharpen it, refine it, give it what it lacks, perfect what it already possesses.

The Mother, 12: 73

Advent of this transformation

Nature is striving towards this new manifestation. But her ways are tortuous and her march is uncertain, full of halts and regressions, so much so that it is difficult to perceive her true plan. However, it is becoming more and more clear that she wants to bring forth a new species out of the human species, a supramental race that will be to man what man is to the animal. But the advent of this transformation, this creation of a new race which Nature would take centuries of groping attempts to bring about, can be effected by the intelligent will of man, not only in a much shorter time but also with much less waste and loss.

The Mother, 12: 98

To succeed in our yoga

Do not forget that to succeed in our yoga one must have a strong and healthy body.

For this, the body must do exercise, have an active and regular life, work physically, eat well, and sleep well.

It is in good health that the way towards transformation is found.

The Mother, 5: 147

Inner harmony

Good health is the exterior expression of an inner harmony. We must be proud if we are in good health and not despise it.

The Mother, 15: 147

Happiness and good health

As yet happiness and good health are not normal conditions in this world.

We must protect them carefully against the intrusion of their opposites.

The Mother, 15: 147

Our forgotten vastnesses

This world is a beginning and a base
Where Life and Mind erect their structured dreams;
An unborn Power must build reality.
A deathbound littleness is not all we are:
Immortal our forgotten vastnesses
Await discovery in our summit selves;
Unmeasured breadths and depths of being are ours.

Sri Aurobindo, 28: 46

An adventure

It can be called an adventure because it is the first
time that a yoga aims at transformation and divinisation
of physical life instead of escape from it.

The Mother, 14: 34

Life on earth

At best, life on earth is a field for progress and one
should take advantage of it as best one can in order to
reach as soon as possible the degree of perfection which
will put an end to the ordeal by making it unnecessary.

The Mother, 12: 48

True Maternity

Supermanhood

The way to supermanhood lies in the unfolding of the ever-perfect Spirit.

The Mother, 2: 161

A new consciousness

...we must first understand... what are the means by which the present chaos and obscurity can be transformed into light and harmony.

Many means have been suggested: political, social, ethical, even religious.... Indeed, none of these seem sufficient to face with any reliable success the magnitude of the task to be done. Only a new spiritual influx, creating in man a new consciousness, can overcome the enormous mass of difficulties barring the way of the workers. A new spiritual light, a manifestation upon earth of some divine force unknown until now, a

Thought of God, new for us, descending into this world and taking a new form here.

And here we come back to our starting point, to our duty of true maternity. For this form meant to manifest the spiritual force capable of transforming the earth's present conditions, this new form, who is to construct it if not the women?

The Mother, 2: 156

Superman

The superman shall be born of woman, this is a big unquestionable truth....

The Mother, 2: 156

Manifesting an ideal

To bear a child and construct his body almost subconsciously is not enough. The work really commences when, by the power of thought and will, we conceive and create a character capable of manifesting an ideal.

The Mother, 2: 153

Birth of the superman

...we must strive to come in touch mentally, by the constant aspiration of our thought and will, with the supreme possibility which, exceeding all human measures and features, will give birth to the superman.

The Mother, 2: 157

Maternity becomes truly precious and sacred

Why accept the obscure bonds of heredity and atavism – which are nothing else than subconscious preferences for our own trend of character – when we can, by concentration and will, call into being a type constructed according to the highest ideal we are able to conceive? With this effort, maternity becomes truly precious and sacred; indeed with this, we enter the glorious work of the Spirit, and womanhood rises above animality and its ordinary instincts, towards real humanity and its powers.

The Mother, 2: 154

Conscious parents

The body is formed by a man and a woman who become the father and mother, and it is they who don't even have the *means* of asking the being they are going to bring into the world whether it would like to come or whether this is in accordance with its destiny. And it is on this body they have formed that they impose by force, by force of necessity, an atavism, an environment, later an education, which will almost always be obstacles to its future growth.

Therefore, I said here and I am repeating it – I thought I had been clear enough – that it was about the physical parents and the physical body I was speaking, nothing else. And that the soul which incarnates, whether it be in course of development or fully developed, has to struggle against the circumstances imposed on it by this animal birth, struggle in order to find its true path and again discover its own self fully.

The Mother, 8: 200

An aspiration

> *Sweet Mother, is it possible for the mother and father to give birth to… to ask for the soul they want?*

To ask? For that they must have an occult knowledge which they don't usually have. But anyway, what is possible is that instead of doing the thing like an animal driven by instinct or desire and most of the time, without even wanting it, they do it at will, with an aspiration, putting themselves in a state of aspiration and almost of prayer, so that the being that they are going to form may be one fit to embody a soul which they *can* call down to incarnate in that form.

The Mother, 8: 201

Calling a soul

It is possible to call a soul, but one must be at least a little conscious oneself, and must want to do what one does in the best conditions. This is very rare, but it is possible.

The Mother, 8: 201

State of consciousness in which the parents are

It is perhaps a subconscious wickedness in the parents. It is said that people throw out their wickedness from themselves by giving it birth in their children. One has always a shadow in oneself. There are people who project this outside — that does not always free them from it, but still perhaps it comforts them! But it is the child who "profits" by it, don't you see? It is quite evident that the state of consciousness in which the parents are at that moment is of capital importance.

The Mother, 5: 412

Rise to the surface

I say: even in the best cases, because of the way in which the body is formed at present, you have to face innumerable difficulties which come more or less from the subconscious, but rise to the surface and against which you have to struggle before you can become completely free and develop normally.

The Mother, 8: 204

Parents have a particular formation

Inevitably, parents have a particular formation, they are particularly healthy or unhealthy; even taking things at their best, they have a heap of atavism, habits, formations in the subconscious and even in the unconscious, which come from their own birth, the environment they

have lived in, their own life; and even if they are remarkable people they have a large number of things
which are quite opposed to the true psychic life – even
the best of them, even the most conscious.

The Mother, 8: 203

Obscure birth

I told you that due to this obscure birth one arrives
with a whole physical baggage of things which generally have to be got rid of, if one truly wants to progress,
and some one has quoted my own sentence which runs
like this:

"You are brought here by force, the environment is
imposed on you by force, the laws of atavism of the
milieu by force..."

The Mother, 8: 200

True maternity

True maternity begins with the conscious creation of
a being, with the willed shaping of a soul coming to
develop and utilise a new body. The true domain of
women is the spiritual.

The Mother, 2: 153

Soul and destiny

Man's hopes and longings build the journeying wheels
That bear the body of his destiny

And lead his blind will towards an unknown goal.
His fate within him shapes his acts and rules;
Its face and form already are born in him,
Its parentage is in his secret soul;
Here Matter seems to mould the body's life
And the soul follows where its nature drives:
Nature and Fate compel his freewill's choice.
But greater spirits this balance can reverse
And make the soul the artist of its fate.

Sri Aurobindo, 29: 465

Reason and not by vital impulses

It is a good thing to begin to learn at an early age that to lead an efficient life and obtain from one's body the maximum it is able to give, reason must be the master of the house. And it is not a question of yoga or higher realisation, it is something which should be taught everywhere, in every school, every family, every home: man was made to be a mental being, and merely to be a man – we are not speaking of anything else, we are speaking only of being a man – life must be dominated by reason and not by vital impulses. This should be taught to all children from their infancy.

The Mother, 9: 100

Transforming one's character

We know by experience that if we go down into the subconscient, lower than the physical consciousness, into the subconscient and even lower still into the inconscient, we can find in ourselves the origin of atavism, of what comes from our early education and the environment in which we lived. And this gives a kind of special characteristic to the individual, to his outer nature, and it is generally believed that we are born like that and we will stay like that. But by going down into the subconscient, into the inconscient, one can trace the origin of this formation and undo what has been done, change the movements and reactions of the ordinary nature by a conscious and deliberate action and thus really transform one's character.

The Mother, 15: 316

Beings

> *Do beings who have been in contact with You in one life always come back to You in their new lives?*

The number of beings who consciously return to a place of their choice is very small.

Those who have returned are mainly the beings who, before leaving their body, asked to return in a new one.

But everything is possible.

The Mother, 17: 370

Flaming pioneers

I saw the Omnipotent's flaming pioneers
Over the heavenly verge which turns towards life
Come crowding down the amber stairs of birth;
Forerunners of a divine multitude

Out of the paths of the morning star they came
Into the little room of mortal life.

Sri Aurobindo, 28: 343

An explanation

"The Divine Mother had said to me that these Omnipotent's flaming pioneers have started coming down. They are souls that have waited for thousands of years for the right time to take rebirth and come down to prepare the world for the Transformation. The Mother further asked me to inform this to all so that any one of Her disciples who is expecting a child could consciously aspire for one of these souls to come into the expected child. This had to be done before the third month of pregnancy as the soul enters the foetus in the third month. The Mother also asked me to warn the expectant mothers who called down such a soul that the child born would not be as other children and would not behave in the way other children behave and so they may have trouble with them. They would have to be patient and understand that the child has a great soul and give it every opportunity to develop."

As recollected by Udar Pinto, a devotee

The new race

The new race shall be governed by intuition, that is to say, direct perception of the divine law within.

The Mother, 2: 159

The Causes

A problem for medical science

We are at a moment of transition in the history of the earth. It is merely a moment in eternal time, but this moment is long compared to human life. Matter is changing in order to prepare itself for the new manifestation, but the human body is not plastic enough and offers resistance; this is why the number of incomprehensible disorders and even diseases is increasing and becoming a problem for medical science.

The remedy lies in union with the divine forces that are at work and a receptivity full of trust and peace which makes the task easier.

The Mother, 16: 421

Fall in resistance

Even from the ordinary external point of view, it has been recognised for a very long time that it is a fall in resistance of the vitality due to immediate moral causes which is always at the origin of an illness. When one is in a normal state of equilibrium and lives in a normal physical harmony, the body has a capacity of resistance, it has within it an atmosphere strong enough to resist illnesses: its most material substance emanates subtle vibrations which have the strength to resist illnesses, even diseases which are called contagious – in fact, all vibrations are contagious, but still, certain diseases are considered as especially contagious. Well, a man who, even from the purely external point of view, is in a state in which his organs function harmoniously and an adequate psychological balance prevails, has at the same time enough resistance for the contagion not to affect him. But if for some reason or other he loses this equilibrium or is weakened by depression, dissatisfaction, moral difficulties or undue fatigue, for instance, this reduces the normal resistance of the body and he is open to the disease. But if we consider someone who is doing yoga, then it is altogether different, in the sense that the causes of disequilibrium are of a different nature and the illness usually becomes the expression of an inner difficulty which has to be overcome.

The Mother, 9: 120

Origin of an illness

The origin of an illness may be in the mind; it may be in the vital; it may be in any of the parts of the being. One and the same illness may be due to a variety of causes; it may spring in different cases from different sources of disharmony. And there may be too an appearance of illness where there is no real illness at all. In that case, if you were sufficiently conscious you will see that there is just a friction somewhere, some halting in the moment and by setting it right you will be cured at once. This kind of malady has no truth in it, even when it seems to have physical effects. It is half made up of imagination and has not the same grip on matter as a true illness.

The Mother, 3: 88

Disharmony in the being

> *But are not illnesses sometimes the result of microbes and not a part of the movement of the Yoga?*

Where does Yoga begin and where does it end? Is not the whole of your life Yoga? The possibilities of illness are always there in your body and around you; you carry within you or there swarm about you the microbes and germs of every disease. How is it that all of a sudden you succumb to an illness which you did not have for years? You will say it is due to a "depression of the vital force". But from where does the depression come? It comes from some disharmony in the being, from a lack of receptivity to the divine forces.

The Mother, 3: 55

No two illnesses are alike

Sweet Mother, if someone falls seriously ill, is this a purely physical phenomenon or is it a difficulty in his spiritual life?

That depends on the person! If it is someone who is doing yoga, it is quite obviously a difficulty in his spiritual life. If it is somebody who is not at all engaged in yoga and who lives an ordinary life in the most ordinary manner, it is an ordinary accident. It depends absolutely on the person. The outer phenomena may be similar, but the inner causes are absolutely different. No two illnesses are alike, though labels are put on diseases and attempts made to group them; but in fact every person is ill in his own way, and his way depends on what he is, on his state of consciousness and the life he leads.

The Mother, 9: 120

The formation of the body

Naturally, the formation of the body is very important in this sense that if, for instance, one is constantly under the influence of a depression, of pessimism, discouragement, a lack of faith and of trust in life, all this enters, so to say, into one's substance, and then some people, when there is the possibility of an accident, never miss it. Every time there is a chance of something happening to them, they catch it, be it an illness or an accident.

The Mother, 6: 2

Full of fears

In life it is the action of the subconscious that has the larger share and it acts a hundred times more power-fully than the conscious parts. The normal human con-dition is a state filled with apprehensions and fears; if you observe your mind deeply for ten minutes, you will find that for nine out of ten it is full of fears – it carries in it fear about many things, big and small, near and far, seen and unseen, and though you do not usually take conscious notice of it, it is there all the same. To be free from all fear can come only by steady effort and discipline.

The Mother, 3: 57

Illness comes from fear

Some of the diseases which are considered most dan-gerous are the easiest to cure; some that are considered as of very little importance can offer the most obstinate resistance.

The sources of an illness are manifold and intricate; each can have a multitude of causes, but always it indi-cates where is the weak part in the being.

Nine-tenths of the danger in an illness comes from fear.

The Mother, 3: 90

Fear acts like a magnet

If you fear an accident, this acts like a magnet draw-
ing the accident towards you. In this sense, it may be
said that it is the result of character. And the same thing
holds for illness. There are people who can move about
among the sick and in places where there are epidemics and never catch a disease. There are others – it is
enough for them to spend an hour with a sick person,
they catch the illness. That too depends on what they
are within themselves.

The Mother, 6: 2

Subconscient fear

In fact, ninety percent of illnesses are the result of the
subconscient fear of the body. In the ordinary consciousness of the body there is a more or less hidden anxiety
about the consequences of the slightest physical disturbance. It can be translated by these words of doubt about
the future: "And what will happen?" It is this anxiety
that must be checked. Indeed this anxiety is a lack of
confidence in the Divine's Grace, the unmistakable sign
that the consecration is not complete and perfect.

The Mother, 15: 151

If your thought is not healthy

If your thought is not healthy, if your feelings and
thoughts are bad so to speak, your nerves become very

bad, still worse. For instance, those who entertain all kinds of unhealthy fancies, those who like unhealthy reading, unhealthy conversations – there are many of this kind, there is a large number of them – well, they may lose all control over their nerves, they may become extremely nervous and yet have a body that's in a fine condition and very healthy.

The Mother, 6: 76

Vital and mental

And if the vital and the mental were left as masters of action, they would simply harass the body, destroy its poise and upset its health.

The Mother, 2: 289

Illness enters the subconscient

For example, there are bad habits of the body, in the sense that the body is in the habit of upsetting its balance – we call that falling ill, you know; but still, the functioning becomes defective through a bad habit. You manage by concentrating the Force and applying it on this defect, to make it disappear but it doesn't disappear completely, it enters the subconscient. And then, when you are off your guard, when you stop paying attention properly and preventing it from showing itself, it rises up and comes out. You thought for months perhaps or even for years, you were completely rid of a certain kind of illness which you suffered from and you no longer paid any attention, and suddenly one day it returns as though it had never gone; it springs up again from the subconscient, and unless one enters into this subconscient and changes things there, that is, unless one changes the subconscient into conscient, it always happens like this.

The Mother, 7: 144

Old habit

This attack [of illness] is not due to work or exposure but to the suggestion of an old habit rising from the subconscient. Do not listen to what people say and keep your faith in the Divine's Grace.

The Mother, 15: 153

Illness is an index

The particular place in the body affected by an illness is an index to the nature of the inner disharmony that has taken place. It points to the origin, it is the sign of the cause of the ailment. It reveals too the nature of the resistance that prevents the whole being from advancing at the same high speed.

The Mother, 3: 88

Greed in the nature

Tumours always indicate some difficulty in the nature; certain cells decide to be independent of the discipline of the body. They do not remain in harmony with the other parts and begin to grow out of all proportion. Generally this is the result of a very strong greed in the nature. It may be greed for material things or for power or any other subtle object.

The Mother, 5: 176

Psychological domain

In the psychological domain, only the patients who do not want to recover do not recover. Perhaps it is the same for physical diseases.

The Mother, 16: 72

Cutting oneself off from the light

When you cut yourself off from the energy and light that sustain you, then there is this depression, there is created what medical science calls a "Favourable ground" and something takes advantage of it. It is doubt, gloominess, lack of confidence, a selfish turning back upon yourself that cuts you off from the light and divine energy and gives the attack this advantage. It is this that is the cause of your falling ill and not microbes.

The Mother, 3: 56

Nervous envelope

There is a sort of protection round the body which we call the nervous envelope – if this remains strong and refuses entrance to the illness force, then one can remain well even in the midst of plague or other epidemics – if the envelope is pierced or weak then the illness can come in.

Sri Aurobindo, 24: 1565

Break in the nervous envelope

They [the subtle forces of illness] first weaken or break through the nervous envelope, the aura. If that is strong and whole, a thousand million germs will not be able to do anything to you. The envelope pierced, they attack the subconscient mind in the body, sometimes also the vital mind or mind proper – prepare the illness by fear or thought of illness.

Sri Aurobindo, 24: 1565

Depression

A bad suggestion acts very strongly upon it; a good suggestion operates in the contrary sense with the same force. Depression and discouragement have a very adverse effect; they cut out holes in it, as it were, in its very stuff, render it weak and unresisting and open to hostile attacks an easy passage.

The Mother, 3: 89

Accidents

Accidents are due to many things; in fact they are the result of a conflict of the forces in nature, a conflict between forces of growth and progress and the forces of destruction. When there is an accident, an accident that has lasting results, it is always the result of a more or less partial victory of the adverse forces, that is, of the forces of disintegration, disorganisation.

The Mother, 6: 1

Anxiety

Say you have the slightest thing that is not getting on quite well; if you think of your body, it is always that something unpleasant is going to happen to it – because when everything goes well, you don't think about it! You will notice this: that you act, you do all that you have to do, without having a single thought about your body, and when all of a sudden you wonder whether there isn't anything that's going wrong, whether there is some uneasiness or a difficulty, something, then you begin to think of your body and you think about it with anxiety and begin to make your disastrous constructions.

The Mother, 7: 5

Desire

In order to be cured, my child, not only is it necessary to stop all these unseemly practices completely, but it is necessary to get rid of all these unhealthy desires from your thought and sensation, for it is desires that irritate the organs and make them ill.

The Mother, 15: 159

Psychological and physical diseases

Psychological diseases are of the thoughts and feelings, such as depression, revolt, sadness, etc. Physical diseases are those of the body.

The Mother, 16: 72

Disharmony

But rapid progress in one part of the being which is not followed by an equivalent progress in other parts produces a disharmony in the nature, a dislocation somewhere; and wherever or whenever this dislocation occurs, it can translate itself into an illness. The nature of the illness depends upon the nature of the dislocation. One kind of disharmony affects the mind and the disturbance it produces may lead even as far as insanity; another kind affects the body and may show itself as fever or prickly heat or any other greater or minor disorder.

The Mother, 3: 86

Psychological state of the body

This body is built up, on the one side, of a material basis, but rather of material conditions than of physical matter, on the other, of the vibrations of our psychological states. Peace and equanimity and confidence, faith in health, undisturbed repose and cheerfulness and bright gladness constitute this element in it and give it strength and substance.

The Mother, 3: 89

Will to illness

By will to illness I meant this that there is something in the body that accepts the illness and has certain reactions that make this acceptance effective – so there must always be a contrary will in the conscious parts of the being to get rid of this most physical acceptance.

Sri Aurobindo, 24: 1567

Old habit of consciousness

What I meant was that the body consciousness through old habit of consciousness admits the force of the illness and goes through the experiences which are associated with it – e.g., congestion of phlegm in the chest and feeling of suffocation or difficulty of breathing, etc.

Sri Aurobindo, 24: 1567

Inertia

All ill-health is due to some inertia or weakness or to some resistance or wrong movement there, only it has sometimes a more physical and sometimes a more psychological character.

Sri Aurobindo, 24: 1567-68

Fatigue

Fatigue comes from doing without interest the things you do.

The Mother, 14: 267

Obscurity

Illness marks some imperfection or weakness or else opening to adverse touches in the physical nature and is often connected also with some obscurity or disharmony in the lower vital or the physical mind or elsewhere.

Sri Aurobindo, 24: 1568

Weakness

The suggestion of weakness comes to the subconscient part of the body consciousness and therefore the mind is most often unaware of it. If the body itself were truly conscious, then the suggestions could be detected in time and thrown off before they took effect. Also the

rejection by the central consciousness would be supported by a conscious rejection in the body and act more
immediately and promptly.

Sri Aurobindo, 24: 1573

Origin of our suffering

A whisper lures to evil the human heart,
It seals up wisdom's eyes, the soul's regard,
It is the origin of our suffering here,
It binds earth to calamity and pain.

Sri Aurobindo, 29: 448

Monkey wiser than man!

And it is simply a perversion, a deformation which
is a denial of the life instinct, it is an unhealthy interfer-
ence of thought and vital impulse in physical life. It is
an unhealthy impulse, it doesn't usually exist even in
animals. In this case, instinct in animals is infinitely more
reasonable than human instinct – which, besides, doesn't
exist anymore, which has been replaced by a very perverted impulse....

There is a story about some officers in North Africa –
in Algeria – who had adopted a monkey. The monkey
lived with them and one day at dinner they had a gro-
tesque idea and gave the monkey something to drink.
They gave it alcohol. The monkey first saw the others
drink, this seemed to it something quite interesting, and
it drank a glass, a full glass of wine. Afterwards it was

ill, as ill as could be, it rolled under the table with all kinds of pains and was really in a very bad way, that is, it gave the men an example of the spontaneous effect of alcohol when the physical nature is not already perverted. It nearly died of poisoning. It recovered. And sometime later it was again allowed to come for dinner as it was alright, and somebody placed a glass of wine in front of it. It picked it up in a terrible rage and flung it at the head of the man who had given the glass to it…. By that it showed that it was much wiser than the men!

The Mother, 9: 100

Disturbance of equilibrium

We have often said that illnesses are always the result of a disturbance of equilibrium, but this disturbance can occur in completely different states of being. For the ordinary man whose consciousness is centred in the physical, outer life, it is a purely physical disturbance of equilibrium, of the functioning of the different organs. But when behind this purely superficial life, an inner life is being fashioned, the causes of illness change; they always become the expression of a disequilibrium between the different parts of the being: between the inner progress or effort and the outer resistances or conditions of one's life, one's body.

The Mother, 9: 120

Fear in the cells

So each one should find out for himself why he is ill.

From the ordinary point of view, in most cases, it is usually fear – fear, which may be mental fear, vital fear, but which is almost always physical fear, a fear in the cells – it is fear which opens the door to all contagion. Mental fear – all who have a little control over themselves, or any human dignity can eliminate it; vital fear is more subtle and asks for a great control; as for physical fear, a veritable yoga is necessary to overcome it, for the cells of the body are afraid of everything that is unpleasant, painful, and as soon as there is any unease, even if it is insignificant, the cells of the body become anxious, they don't like to be uncomfortable. And then, to overcome that, the control of a conscious will is necessary. It is usually this kind of fear that opens the door to illnesses…. But physical fear is more difficult to overcome; without it even the most violent attacks could be repelled. If one has a minimum of control over the body, one can lessen its effects, but that is not immunity. It is this kind of trembling of material, physical fear in the cells of the body which aggravates all illnesses.

The Mother, 9: 121

Force of disintegration

For every indisposition, every illness, every malformation, even accidents, are the result of the action of the force of disintegration, just as growth, harmonious development, resistance to attack, recovery from illness, every return to the normal functioning, every progressive improvement, are due to the action of the force of transformation.

The Mother, 12: 86

Fear

But when one can eliminate fear, one is almost in safety. For example, epidemics, or so–called epidemics, like those which are raging at present – ninety-nine times out of a hundred they come from fear: a fear, then, which even becomes a mental fear in its most sordid form, promoted by newspaper articles, useless talk and so on.

The Mother, 9: 122

Break in equilibrium

I have told you first of all that all illness without any exception – without exception – is the expression of a break in equilibrium. But there are many kinds of breaks in equilibrium.... First, I am speaking only of the body, I am not speaking of the nervous illnesses of the vital or of mental illnesses. We shall see that later on. We are speaking only of this poor little body. And I say that all illnesses, all, whatever they may be (I would add even accidents) come from a break in equilibrium. That is, if all your organs, all the members and parts of your body are in harmony with one another, you are in perfect health. But if there is the slightest imbalance anywhere, immediately you get either just a little ill or quite ill, even very badly ill, or else an accident occurs. That always happens whenever there is an inner imbalance.

The Mother, 5: 173

Mind intervenes

Human beings have a much more delicate and precarious health than animals because their mind intervenes and disturbs the equilibrium. The body, left to itself, has a very sure instinct. For instance, never will the body if left to itself eat when it doesn't need to or take something which will be harmful to it. And it will sleep when it needs to sleep, it will act when it needs to act. The instinct of the body is very sure. It is the vital and the mind which disturb it: one by its desires and caprices, the other by its principles, dogmas, laws and ideas. And unfortunately, in civilisation as it is understood, with the kind of education given to children, this sure instinct of the body is completely destroyed: it is the rest that dominate. And naturally things happen as they do: one eats things that are harmful, one doesn't take rest when one needs to or sleeps too much when it is not necessary or does things one shouldn't do and spoils one's health completely.

The Mother, 5: 295

Slightest scratch

The vital body surrounds the physical body with a kind of envelope which has almost the same density as the vibrations of heat observable when the day is very hot. And it is this which is the intermediary between the subtle body and the most material vital body. It is this which protects the body from all contagion, fatigue, exhaustion and even from accidents. Therefore if this envelope is wholly intact, it protects you from everything, but a little too strong an emotion, a little fatigue, some dissatisfaction or any shock whatsoever is sufficient to scratch it as it were and the slightest scratch allows any kind of intrusion. Medical science also now recognises that if you are in perfect vital equilibrium, you do not catch illness or in any case you have a kind of immunity from contagion.

The Mother, 4: 63

Always wavering

Once you have chosen the path, you must boldly accept all the consequences of your choice. But if you choose and then draw back and choose again and again draw back, always wavering, always doubting, always fearful, you create a disharmony in your being, which not only retards your progress, but can be the origin of all kinds of disturbance in the mind and vital being and discomfort and disease in the body.

The Mother, 3: 91

Dislocation in the system

The body, on the other hand, is ordinarily dense, inert and apathetic. And if you have in this part something that is not responsive, if there is a resistance here, the reason is that the body is incapable of moving as quickly as the rest of the being. It must take time, it must walk at its own pace as it does in ordinary life. What happens is as when grown-up people walk too fast for children in their company; they have to stop at times and wait till the child who is lagging behind comes up and overtakes them. This divergence between the progress in the inner being and the inertia of the body often creates a dislocation in the system, and that manifests itself as an illness.

The Mother, 3: 86

Obstinate Sanskaras

In the subconscient there is an obscure mind full of obstinate Sanskaras, impressions, associations, fixed notions, habitual reactions formed by our past, an obscure vital full of the seeds of habitual desires, sensations and nervous reactions, a most obscure material which governs much that has to do with the condition of the body. It is largely responsible for our illnesses; chronic or repeated illnesses are indeed mainly due to the subconscient and its obstinate memory and habit of repetition of whatever has impressed itself upon the body-consciousness.

Sri Aurobindo, 22: 353

Wrong thinking

In fact I can assure you that the pain in the stomach as well as many other discomforts are due 90% to wrong thinking and strong imaginations – I mean that the material basis for them is practically negligible.

The Mother, 15: 155

You must change

Your illness was not a mere accident. You did not give sufficient attention to the inner change, a psychological change with a broadening of your consciousness. You were satisfied with yourself. You were shut up in your small shell and did not try to make any progress. You said sadhana did not interest you and you thought that the little work that you were doing was quite sufficient for you and nothing more was needed. It was this attitude that took you out of my protection. I gave you a warning, but you challenged Nature by saying that nothing could touch you. All these things combined and brought your mental difficulties, weakness and illness.

You must change.

The Mother, 15: 149-50

The Ways:
Personal Effort

Faith in health

To whatever cause an illness may be due, material or mental, external or internal, it must, before it can affect the physical body, touch another layer of the being that surrounds and protects it. This subtler layer is called in different teachings by various names, – the etheric body, the nervous envelope. It is a subtle body and yet almost visible. In density something like the vibrations that you see around a very hot and steaming object, it emanates from the physical body and closely covers it…. It is a perfect protection against all possible attacks of illness, so long as it is whole and entire, thoroughly consistent in its composition, its elements in faultless balance. This body is built up, on one side, of a material basis, but rather of material conditions than of physical matter, on the other, of the vibrations of our psychological states. Peace and equanimity and confidence, faith in health, undisturbed repose and cheerfulness and bright glad-

ness constitute this element in it and give it strength
and substance.

The Mother, 3: 89

Throw the illness away

Attacks of illness are attacks of the lower nature or of
adverse forces taking advantage of some weakness,
opening or response in the nature, – like all other things
that come and have got to be thrown away, they come
from outside. If one can feel them so coming and get
the strength and the habit to throw them away before
they can enter the body, then one can remain free from
illness.

Sri Aurobindo, 24: 1564

Prevent an illness

All illnesses pass through the nervous or vital-physi-
cal sheath of the subtle consciousness and subtle body
before they enter the physical. If one is conscious of the
subtle body or with the subtle consciousness, one can
stop an illness on its way and prevent it from entering
the physical body.

Sri Aurobindo, 24: 1564

Stop illness

Sweet Mother, when one sees an illness coming, how can one stop it?

Ah! First of all, you must not want it, and nothing in the body must want it. You must have a very strong will not to be ill. This is the first condition.

The Mother, 7: 144

Reinforce the nervous envelope

But if we develop the inward physical consciousness, we become aware of a subtle environmental physical atmosphere and can feel the forces of illness coming towards us through it, feel them even at a distance and, if we have learnt how to do it, we can stop them by the will or otherwise. We sense too around us a vital physical or nervous envelope which radiates from the body and protects it, and we can feel the adverse forces trying to break through it and can interfere, stop them or reinforce the nervous envelope. Or we can feel the symptoms of illness, fever or cold, for instance, in the subtle physical sheath before they are manifest in the gross body and destroy them there, preventing them from manifesting in the body. Take now the call for the Divine Power, Light, Ananda. If we live only in the outward physical consciousness, it may descend and work behind the veil, but we shall feel nothing and only see certain results after a long time.

Sri Aurobindo, 22: 350

Not to be afraid

When physical disorder comes, one must not be afraid; one must not run away from it, must face it with courage, calmness, confidence, with the certitude that illness is a *falsehood* and that if one turns entirely, in full confidence, with a complete quietude to the divine grace, it will settle in these cells as it establishes itself in the depths of the being, and the cells themselves will share in the eternal Truth and Delight.

The Mother, 15: 152

Not to worry

My advice is not to worry. The more you think of it, the more you concentrate upon it and, above all, the more you fear, the more you give a chance for the thing to grow.

If, on the contrary, you turn your attention and your interest elsewhere you increase the possibilities of cure.

The Mother, 15: 154

Unfailing method

The only unfailing method for getting rid of illnesses is to turn one's attention away from them and refuse to give them any importance.

The Mother, 17: 92

Turn one's attention away

... there is one thing that one can try to do: it is not to concentrate on one's pain, to turn the attention away as much as possible, not think at all of one's pain, think as little as possible and above all not be concentrated on it, not to pay attention — "Oh, I'm in pain", then it becomes a little worse; "Oh, I'm in still greater pain", then it becomes still worse, like that, because one is concentrated on it; and this is the mistake one always makes: to think, be there, attentive, awaiting the sign of pain; then naturally it comes, it comes increased by the concentration of the attention given to it. That is why, when one is not well the best thing to do is to read or have something read, you see; it depends on the condition one is in. But if one can turn one's attention away, one no longer suffers.

The Mother, 7: 131

True attitude

But the true attitude when one is ill, is to say: "There is something that is not all right; I am going to see what it is." You must never think that the Divine has purposely sent an illness, for that would truly be a very undesirable Divine.

The Mother, 15: 171

The pain vanishes

If the consciousness is turned upward, the pain va-
nishes. If it is turned downward, the pain is felt and
even increases.

The Mother, 15: 156

Thrown away illness

Attacks of illness are attacks of the lower nature or of
adverse forces taking advantage of some weakness,
opening or response in the nature, – like all other things
that come and have got to be thrown away, they come
from outside.

Sri Aurobindo, 24: 1564

If ever you have a headache

... if ever you have a headache I advise you to do
this: to take the thought-force, the mental force and even
if you can draw a little of your vital force, that too and
make it come down, like this (*gesture of very slowly slid-
ing both hands from the top of the head downwards*). Well, if
you have a headache or a congestion, if you have caught
a touch of the sun, for instance, indeed if anything has
happened to you, well, if you know how to do this and
bring down the force here, like this, here (*showing the
centre of the chest*), or even lower down (*showing the stomach*), well, it will disappear. It will disappear. You will
be able to do this in five minutes. You can try, the next

time you have a headache.... I hope you won't have a headache but the next time you have it, try this. Sit upright, like this (*movement showing an asana posture*). The Japanese say you should sit on your heels but that might disturb your meditation, sitting like that they call it sitting at ease. The Indian fashion is like this (*gesture*), otherwise you must sit like this (*gesture*); this is harder when you are not accustomed to it.

The Mother, 6: 312

Infusing consciousness into the cells

Gradually,... you must, with a methodical work of infusing consciousness into the cells of the body, infuse at the same time the truth of the divine Presence. This work takes time, but, if done methodically and constantly, it produces an effect.

So you have prepared the ground.

Suppose that as a result of some illness or other, there is some sort of pain at a precise spot. At that moment all will depend, as I said at the beginning, on the approach most familiar to you. But we can give an example. You are in pain, in great pain; it is hurting very much, you are suffering a lot.

First point: do not stress the pain by telling yourself, "Oh, how painful! Oh, this pain is unbearable! Oh, it is becoming worse and worse, I shall never be able to bear it", etc., all this sort of thing. The more you go on thinking like this and feeling like this and the more your attention is concentrated on it, the pain increases amazingly.

So, the first point: to control yourself sufficiently not to do that.

Second point: as I said, it depends on your habits. If you know how to concentrate, to be quiet, and if you can bring into yourself a certain peace, of any kind – it may be a mental peace, it may be a vital peace, it may be a psychic peace; they have different values and qualities, this is an individual question – you try to realise within yourself a state of peace or attempt to enter into a conscious contact with a force of peace…. Suppose you succeed more or less completely. Then, if you can draw the peace into yourself and bring it down into the solar plexus – for we are not talking of inner states but of your physical body – and from there direct it very calmly, very slowly I might say, but very persistently, towards the place where the pain is more or less sharp, and fix it there, this is very good.

This is not always enough.

But if by widening this movement you can add a sort of mental formation with a little life in it – not just cold, but with a little life in it – that the only reality is the divine Reality, and all the cells of this body are a more or less deformed expression of this divine Reality – there is only one Reality, the Divine, and our body is a more or less deformed expression of this sole Reality – if by my aspiration, my concentration, I can bring into the cells of the body the consciousness of this *sole* Reality, all disorder must necessarily cease.

If you can add to that a movement of complete and trusting surrender to the Grace, then I am sure that within five minutes your suffering will disappear. If you know how to do it.

You may try and yet not succeed. But you must know how to try again and again and again, until you do succeed. But if you do those three things at the same time, well, there is no pain which can resist.

. The Mother, 8: 213-14

Turn toward the Divine

I say "turn upward" because to turn toward the Divine is the best method, but what can be said in general is that if the consciousness is turned away from the pain to one's work or anything that interests one, the pain ceases.

The Mother, 15: 157

Remain normal

When I was twenty, a doctor told me that in cases of troubles of the stomach or intestines, the best thing is to continue eating as usual and not to bother about the trouble. He said, "If you have acidity, it will come from whatever food you take and the more you bother about it, the more it will increase. If you go on changing your food, in the end you will find that you cannot even drink a drop of water without getting into trouble. But if you remain normal and don't worry, you will become all right"

And I have found this advice to be quite true.

The Mother, 15: 155

The will and faith

For nearly forty years I suffered constantly from the smaller and the greater ailments, behind the wholly good I was weakly in constitution and mistook their cure for a burden that Nature had laid upon me. When I renounced the aid of medicines, then they began to depart from me like disappointed parasites. Then only I understood what a mighty force was the natural health within me and how much mightier yet the Will and Faith exceeding mind which God meant to be the divine support of our life in the body.

Sri Aurobindo, 17: 125

Will to conquer

Wake up in yourself a will to conquer. Not a mere will in the mind but a will in the very cells of your body. Without that you can't do anything; you may take a hundred medicines but they won't cure you unless you have a will to overcome the physical illness.

The Mother, 15: 158

No reason to be ill

Why imagine always that one is ill or is going to be ill and thus open oneself to all kinds of bad suggestions? There is no reason to be ill and I don't see why you should be so.

The Mother, 16: 194

Conquer the difficulty

> *If I could detach myself entirely from this outer world,*
> *if I could be quite alone, I would master this depression*
> *which I cannot shake off.*

This is not at all correct; the experience of all recluses, all ascetics, proves indisputably the contrary. The difficulty comes from oneself, from one's own nature, and one takes it along wherever one goes, whatever the conditions one may be in. There is but one way of getting out of it – it is to conquer the difficulty, overcome one's lower nature.

The Mother, 16: 190

Purify

Certainly it is better to purify one's mind and purify one's vital before thinking of purifying one's body. For even if you take all possible precautions and live physically taking care not to absorb anything except what will help to subtilise your body, if your mind and vital remain in a state of desire, inconscience, darkness, passion and all the rest, that won't be of any use at all. Only, your body will become weak, dislocated from the inner life and one fine day it will fall ill.

The Mother, 6: 180

Purify the higher and then purify the lower

One must begin from inside, I have already told you
this once. One must begin from above, first purify the
higher and then purify the lower. I am not saying that
one must indulge in all sorts of degrading things in the
body. That's not what I am telling you. Don't take it as
an advice not to exercise control over your desires! It
isn't that at all. But what I mean is, do not try to be an
angel in the body if you are not already just a little of an
angel in your mind and vital; for that would dislocate
you in a different way from the usual one, but not one
that is better. We said the other day that what is most
important is to keep the equilibrium.

The Mother, 6: 180

Repeat to yourself

... It was in this way that he cured his patients; he
was a doctor, he told them, "You are going to repeat to
yourself: 'I am being cured, gradually I am getting
cured' and again, you see, 'I am strong, I am quite
healthy and I can do this, I can do that.' "

The Mother, 7: 5

Infusing confidence into the cells

First, not to want to be ill, and then not to be afraid
of illness. You must neither attract it nor tremble. You
must not want illness at all. But you must not because

of fear not want it; you must not be afraid; you must have a calm certitude and a complete trust in the power of the Grace to shelter you from everything, and then think of something else, not be concerned about this any longer. When you have done these two things, refusing the illness with all your will and infusing a confidence which completely eliminates the fear in the cells of the body, and then busying yourself with something else, not thinking any longer about the illness, forgetting that it exists... there, if you know how to do that, you may even be in contact with people who have contagious diseases, and yet you do not catch them. But you must know how to do this.

The Mother, 7: 145

Saying to the nerve...

But my own method which consists in saying to the nerve, "Now you have done your job, keep quiet, you don't need to tell me anything more", is much better. One cuts it and then it's over.

The Mother, 7: 150

Transform pain

Sweet Mother, how can one transform pain into forms of pleasure?

... For example, you have cut your finger, there's a nerve that has been affected, and so the nerve quickly goes to tell the brain, up there, that something has happened which is wrong, here. That is what gives you the pain to awaken your attention, to tell you: "You know, there's something wrong." Then the thought immediately feels anxious: "What is wrong? Oh! how it hurts", etc., etc. – then returns to the finger and tries to arrange what is not yet destroyed. Usually one puts a small bandage. But in order not to have the pain, if it hurts very much, you must quite simply cut the connection by thought, saying to the nerve, "Now remain quiet, you have done your work, you have warned me, you don't need to say anything any longer; ploff! I am stopping you." And when you do it well, you suffer no longer, it is finished, you stop the pain completely. That is the best thing. It is infinitely preferable to telling yourself that it is painful.

The Mother, 7: 149

Change of character

I do not believe in a change [of place]. It is for him a question of nature and temperament and wherever he goes that will necessarily go with him. It is only a change of character obtained by sadhana that can cure him.

The Mother, 17: 399

Auto suggestion

These auto-suggestions – it is really faith in a mental form – act both on the subliminal and the subconscient.

In the subliminal they set in action the powers of the inner being, its occult power to make thought, will or simple conscious force effective on the body – in the subconscient they silence or block the suggestions of death and illness (expressed or unexpressed) that prevent the return of health. They help also to combat the same things (adverse suggestions) in the mind, vital, body consciousness. Where all this is completely done or with some completeness, the effects can be very remarkable.

Sri Aurobindo, 24: 1589

Not to give value to illness

Your ailment is evidently in its foundation an illness of the nerves and not an ordinary physical disease. ... they increase if anything in you assents to them and accepts, and the more the mind gives value to them and dwells on them, the more they grow. The only way is to remain quiet, dissociate yourself and refuse to accept it or make much of it, allow the calm and strength that the Mother has been putting around you to enter your mind and permeate your nervous system.

Sri Aurobindo, 24: 1343

Not to love ill health

Do not love your ill health and the ill health will leave you.

The Mother, 15: 158

Be patient

The physical nature is obscure and recalcitrant everywhere; it is very difficult for it to become conscious of the divine Presence.

That is why we must be patient and keep on aspiring with the certitude of Victory.

The Mother, 14: 383

Power of imagination

Every time you indulge your imagination in an unhealthy way, giving a form to your fears and anticipating accidents and misfortunes, you are undermining your own future. On the other hand, the more optimistic your imagination, the greater the chance of your realising your aim. Monsieur Coué got hold of this potent truth and cured hundreds of people by simply teaching them to imagine themselves out of misery. He once related the case of a lady whose hair was falling off. She began to suggest to herself that she was improving every day and that her hair was surely growing. By constantly imagining it her hair really began to grow and even reached an enviable length owing to still further autosuggestion.

The Mother, 3: 156

Microbes that cure

Now, quite recently, they have found something else

and I consider it wonderful. They have discovered that for every disease there is a microbe that cures it (call it a microbe if you like, anyway, some sort of germ). But what is so extraordinary is that this "microbe" is extremely contagious, even more contagious than the microbe of the disease. And it generally develops under two conditions: in those who have a sort of good natural good humour and energy and those who have a strong will to get well! Suddenly they catch the "microbe" and are cured. And what is wonderful is that if there is one who is cured in an epidemic, three more recover immediately. And this "microbe" is found in all who are cured.

The Mother, 4: 210

Concentrate

With your blessings my disease gets partially cured but does not go.

This gives the exact measure of your body's receptivity. Concentrate the force on the diseased parts and they will improve.

The Mother, 15: 166

Call the light

It is not very difficult to get rid of headache and giddiness. However bad your condition may be, call the light from above. Try to feel that the light is entering into you from the crown of your head bringing with it calm and peace. If you do it seriously, your headache and giddiness will disappear in no time.

The Mother, 15: 176

Cancer can be cured

The cells of the body get the habit of increasing without cause. This is cancer. If you change the consciousness in the cells and get rid of their habit, cancer can be cured.

The Mother, 15: 177

Harmony or disorder

> *Sweet Mother,*
> *Are illnesses and accidents the result of something bad one has thought or done, of a fall in one's consciousness? If the cause is a mistake one has made, how can one find out what it is?*

It has nothing to do with punishment; it is the natural and normal consequence of an error, shortcoming or fault which necessarily has consequences. Actually, everything in the world is a question of equilibrium or disequilibrium, of harmony or disorder. Vibrations of harmony attract and encourage harmonious events; vibrations of disequilibrium create, as it were, a disequilibrium in circumstances (illnesses, accidents, etc.). This may be collective or individual, but the principle is the same and so is the remedy: to cultivate in oneself order and harmony, peace and equilibrium by surrendering unreservedly to the Divine Will.

The Mother, 16: 323

Bring down peace

Bring down peace, the Divine Peace in your stomach and it will be all right.

The Mother, 17: 316

Calm, equanimity and endurance

...It is true also that one must be able to bear illness with calm, equanimity, endurance, even recognition of it, since it has come, as something that had to be passed through in the course of experience. But to accept and enjoy it means to help it to last and that will not do; for illness is a deformation of the physical nature just as lust, anger, jealousy, etc., are deformation of the vital nature and error and prejudice and indulgence of false-hood are deformation of the mental nature. All these things have to be eliminated and rejection is the first condition of their disappearance while acceptance has a contrary effect altogether.

Sri Aurobindo, 24: 1566

Aspire to love and peace

> O mortal, bear this great world's law of pain,
> In thy hard passage through a suffering world
> Lean for thy soul's support on Heaven's strength,
> Turn towards high Truth, aspire to love and peace.

Sri Aurobindo, 29: 451

Put light there

> *I have been having various kinds of small accidents and hurts, and I feel troubled because all my efforts to avoid them seem to go in vain. What should I do?*

You need not torture yourself about these small things – they have no importance in themselves and their utility is to show us where inconscience is still to be found in our nature so that we may put light there.

The Mother, 15: 148

The inner consecration

You must take this illness as a sign that in spite of all your convictions, perhaps even resolutions, you have to do sadhana and to add to your outer consecration in work the inner consecration of deep understanding and psychological transformation and make use of your seclusion for that purpose.

My love and help are with you.

The Mother, 15: 148

Be confident

> *What to do about illness?*

Be passively confident: let me do it and it is done.

The Mother, 15: 164

How to pray

> *When one is caught in an illness, how should one pray to the Mother?*

Cure me, O Mother!

The Mother, 15: 164

Strong aspiration

Things that do not want to change in your nature join together and come out in the form of illness. The only thing to be done is to have a strong aspiration and a total change. Then everything will be all right.

The Mother, 15: 150

Clean up everything

You must ruthlessly clean up everything and your will is not strong enough for that; invoke my will, call it sincerely and it will be there to help you. You are right when you say that with my help you will surely be able to conquer. That is true, but you must sincerely want this help and let it work within you and in all circumstances.

The Mother, 15: 159

Illnesses are never serious

Do not let the doctor's words disturb you. Illnesses are never serious unless we accept them as such. Besides, I expect to hear very soon that you are better.

The Mother, 17: 193

Spiritual attitude

Even in the ordinary life disquietude and depression create an unhelpful atmosphere for one who is ill or in difficulties. Once you are a sadhak, then whether for yourself or to help others for whom you still feel, the true spiritual attitude of reliance on the Divine Will and call for the help from above is always the best and most effective course.

Sri Aurobindo, 23: 831

As few as possible

No, not necessary; as few doctors as possible, as few medicines as possible!!

The Mother, 17: 195

Untiring persistence

Certainly, one can act from within on an illness and cure it. Only it is not always easy as there is much resistance in Matter, a resistance of inertia. An untiring persistence is necessary; at first one may fail altogether or the symptoms increase, but gradually the control of the body or of a particular illness becomes stronger.

Sri Aurobindo, 24: 1569

Keep the mind away

The only thing I can suggest about diseases is to call down peace. Keep the mind away from the body by whatever means – whether by reading Sri Aurobindo's books or meditation. It is in this state that the Grace acts. And it is the Grace alone that cures. The medicines only give a faith to the body. That is all.

The Mother, 15: 161

A reasonable person

Most people, when something troubles them, become very unreasonable. When, for example, they are ill, they pass their time saying, "Oh, how ill I am, how frightful it is; is it going to last like that all the time?" And naturally it gets worse and worse. Or when some misfortune befalls them, they cry out: "It is only to me that these things happen and I was thinking that everything was fine before", and they burst into a fit of tears, a fit of nerves. Well, not to speak of superman, in man himself there is a higher capacity called reason, which is able to look at things calmly, coolly, reasonably. And this reason tells you, "Don't worry, that will improve nothing, you must not grumble, you must accept the thing since it has come." Then you immediately become calm. It is a very good mental training, it develops judgment, vision, objectivity and at the same time it has a very healthy action upon your character. It helps you to avoid the ridiculousness of giving way to your nerves and lets you behave like a reasonable person.

The Mother, 4: 46

Put the force and the light

If one could perfectly understand where the mistake is, find out what has been unreceptive, open that part and put the force and the light there, it would be possible to re-establish in a moment the harmony that has been disturbed and the illness would immediately go.

The Mother, 3: 88

Establish peace and quietness

Establish a greater peace and quietness in your body, that will give you the strength to resist attacks of illness.

The Mother, 15: 161

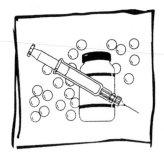

The Ways:
Medicine

Medicine

Medicine is not exactly science. It is theory and experimental fumbling and luck.

Sri Aurobindo, 24:1585

Unshakable faith

One must have an unshakable faith to be able to do without medicines.

The Mother, 16: 195

Taking medicines

... some people can make the effort once, but the second time they no longer do it well, and the third time they don't do it at all; and they tell you, "Oh! one can't be cured by occult means, the divine Force doesn't cure you, it is better to take medicines." So for these, it is better to go to the doctor because this means that they have no spiritual perseverance and only material means can convince them of their effectiveness

The Mother, 7:104

Aid of physical means

It is a fact of my experience that when the resistance in the body is too strong and persistent, it can help to take some aid of physical means as an instrumentation for the Force to work more directly on the body itself; for the body then feels itself supported against the resistance from both sides, by means both physical as well as supraphysical. The Mother's force can work through both together.

Sri Aurobindo, 25: 353-54

Using medicines

Medicines are a *pis aller* that have to be used when something in the consciousness does not respond or responds superficially to the Force.

Sri Aurobindo, 24: 1570

Believing in medicines

Moreover, many facts of knowledge have exactly the same origin. For instance, if a certain medicine, through a concurrence of favorable circumstances, has cured a number of people, immediately it is proclaimed that this medicine is all-powerful against this disease. But it is not true. And the proof is that if the same medicine is administered in the same way to a hundred people, there won't be two similar results, and sometimes the effects will be diametrically opposite. Therefore, it is not the property of the medicine itself which cures; to believe in this medicine is superstition.

The Mother, 8: 92

Self-cure

It should take long for self-cure to replace medicine, because of the fear, self-distrust and unnatural physical reliance on drugs which Medical Science has taught to our minds and bodies and made our second nature.

Sri Aurobindo, 17: 128

Need for medicine

Medicine is necessary for our bodies in disease only because our bodies have learned the art of not getting well without medicines. Even so, one sees often that the moment Nature chooses for recovery is that in which the life is abandoned as hopeless by the doctors.

Sri Aurobindo, 17: 128

Medical Science

Medical Science to the human body is like a great Power which enfeebles a smaller State by its protection

or like a benevolent robber who knocks his victim flat
and riddles him with wounds in order that he may de-
vote his life to healing and serving the shattered body.

Sri Aurobindo, 17: 128

Hits and misses

The doctor aims a drug at a disease; sometimes it hits,
sometimes misses. The misses are left out of account,
the hits treasured up, reckoned and systematised into a
science.

Sri Aurobindo, 17: 126

Distrust

Distrust of the curative power within us was our
physical fall from Paradise. Medical Science and a bad
heredity are the two angels of God who stand at the
gates to forbid our return and re-entry.

Sri Aurobindo, 17:128

Drugs

Drugs cure the body when they do not merely trouble or poison it, but only if their physical attack on the
disease is supported by the force of the spirit; if that
force can be made to work freely, drugs are superflu-
ous.

Sri Aurobindo, 17: 128

Value of a medicine

The whole value of a medicine is in the Spirit it contains.

The Mother, 15: 169

Trust

Medicines have little effect; it is the faith in medicines that cures.

Get treated by the doctor whom you trust and take only the medicines that inspire trust in you.

The body only has trust in material methods and that is why you have to give it medicines – but medicines have an effect only if the Force acts through them.

The Mother, 15: 170

Strike at the psycho-physical root

If one can strike at their psycho-physical root, one can cure even without knowing the pathological whole of the matter and working through the symptoms as a possibility. Some medicines invented by demi-mystics have this power. What I am now considering is whether homeopathy has any psycho-physical basis. Was the founder a demi-mystic? I don't understand otherwise certain peculiarities of the way in which X's medicines act.

Sri Aurobindo, 26: 214

Orthodox and heterodox

I have put down a few comments to throw cold water in all this blazing hot allopathism. But all these furious disputes seem to me now of little use. I have seen the working of both the systems and of others and I can't believe in the sole truth of any. The ones damnable in the orthodox view, entirely contradicting it, have their own truth and succeed – also both the orthodox and heterodox fail.

Sri Aurobindo, 26: 214

Successes and failures

Allopathy, homeopathy, naturopathy, osteopathy, Kaviraji, Hakimi have all caught hold of Nature and subjected her to certain processes; each has its successes and failures. Let each do its work in its own way. I do not see any need for fights and recriminations. For me all are only outward means and what really works are unseen forces from behind; as they act, the outer means succeed or fail – if one can make the process a right channel for the right force, then the process gets its full vitality – that's all.

Sri Aurobindo, 26: 215

Faith and yoga-power

It is very good if one can get rid of illness entirely by faith and yoga-power or the influx of the Divine Force. But very often this is not altogether possible, because the whole nature is not open or able to respond to Force. The mind may have faith and respond, but the lower vital and the body may not follow. Or, if the mind and vital are ready, the body may not respond, or may respond partially, because it has the habit of replying to the forces which produce a particular illness, and habit is a very obstinate force in the material part of the nature. In such cases the use of the physical means can be resorted to, – not as the main means, but as a help or material support to the action of the Force.

Sri Aurobindo, 24: 1568

Call the Mother's Force

To separate yourself from the thing and call in the Mother's Force to cure it – or else to use your will force with faith in the power to heal, having the support of the Mother's Force behind you. If you cannot use either of these methods then you must rely on the action of the medicines.

Sri Aurobindo, 24: 1569

Do not rely on medicines alone

Where the illness becomes pronounced and chronic in the body, it is necessary often to call in the aid of physical treatment and that is then used as a support of the Force. X in his treatment does not rely on medicines alone, but uses them as an instrumentation for the Mother's force.

Sri Aurobindo, 24: 1569

Sometimes a necessity

As for medical treatment it is sometimes a necessity. If one can cure by the Force as you have often done it is best – but if for some reason the body is not able to respond to the Force (e.g. owing to doubt, lassitude or discouragement or for inability to react against the disease), then the aid of medical treatment becomes necessary. It is not that the Force ceases to act and leaves all to the medicines, – it will continue to act through the consciousness but take the support of the treatment so as to act directly on the resistance in the body, which responds more readily to physical means in its ordinary consciousness.

Sri Aurobindo, 24: 1573

Enlightened remedies

> *Sweet Mother,*
> *As soon as You pointed out to me that my heart-condition was getting progressively worse, I stopped taking my present medicine, thinking, "I will take only what the Mother tells me to take." But if you want me not to take any medicine at all and to open myself exclusively to Your Omnipotence, I will do so gladly.*

The body needs to be cared for with physical but enlightened remedies.

The Mother, 17: 355

Use of the medicines

Mother, how are medicines to be used for a body which is not altogether unconscious? For even when we draw on the divine grace, we see that we need a little medicine, and if a little medicine is given it has a good effect. Does it mean that only the body needs medicine or is there something wrong with the mind and the vital?

In most cases the use of medicines – within reasonable limits, that is, when one doesn't poison oneself by taking medicines – is simply to help the body to have confidence. It is the body which heals itself. When it wants to be cured, it is cured. And this is something very widely recognised now; even the most traditional doctors tell you, "Yes, our medicines help, but it is not the medicines which cure, it is the body which decides to be cured." Very well, so when the body is told, "Take this", it says to itself, "Now I am going to get better", and because it says "I am going to get better", well, it is cured!

The Mother, 9: 122

Something else is needed

Mother, by a mental effort – for instance, the resolution not to take medicines when one is ill – can one succeed in making the body understand?

That is not enough. A mental resolution is not

enough, no. There are subtle reactions in your body which do not obey the mental resolution, it is not enough. Something else is needed.

Other regions must be contacted. A power higher than the mind's is needed.

And from this point of view, all that is in the mind is always subject to inner questioning. You take a resolution but you can be sure that something will always come in which perhaps may not openly fight this resolution but will question its effectiveness. It is enough, you see, to be subject to the least doubt for the resolution to lose half its effect. If at the same time as you say "I want", there is something silently lurking, somewhere behind, in the background, something which asks itself, "What will the result be?" that is enough to ruin everything.

The Mother, 9: 123-24

Force acts

In every case, it is the Force that cures.

Medicines have little effect; it is the faith in medicines that cures.

The body only has trust in material methods and that is why you have to give it medicines – but medicines have an effect only if the Force acts through them.

The Mother, 15: 170

Unless it is...

My advice is that medicines should not be used unless it is absolutely impossible to avoid them; and this "absolutely impossible" should be very strict.

The Mother, 12: 15

Not open and awake

If a sadhak can call down the force to cure him without need of medical treatment, that is always the best, but it is not always possible so long as the whole consciousness, mental, vital, physical down to the most subconscient is not open and awake.

Sri Aurobindo, 24: 1568

The Ways:
Doctors

A perfect doctor

A broad mind, a generous heart, and unflinching will, a quiet steady determination, and inexhaustible energy and a total trust in one's mission – this makes a perfect doctor.

The Mother, 15: 167

Power of thought

I have a notion that much protein and starchy food aggravate eczema.

In the effect of food on the body 90% belongs to the power of thought. If you follow with confidence the treatment of Dr. X, it will cure you.

The Mother, 15: 156

Confidence in the doctor

Let him choose his doctor, because it is the confidence in the doctor that is most important.

The Mother, 17: 403

Illnesses are falsehoods of the body

Thus it can be said that illnesses are falsehoods of the body and, consequently, doctors are soldiers of the great and noble army fighting in the world for the conquest of Truth.

The Mother, 15: 167

The chief role

After all, an illness is only a wrong attitude taken by some part of the body.

The chief role of the doctor is, by various means, to induce the body to recover its trust in the Supreme Grace.

The Mother, 15: 167

Medical career is a priesthood

If we take the human body as a tabernacle of the Lord, then medical science becomes the ritual of worship and doctors the priests who officiate in the temple.

Thus considered, the medical career is a priesthood and should be treated as such.

The Mother, 15: 167

Faith in the Divine's Grace

To medical knowledge and experience, add full faith in the Divine's Grace and your healing capacity will have no limits.

The Mother, 15: 167

Do what he asks

I sent you to the doctor and expect you to do what he asks you to do.

The Mother, 15: 169

Spiritual power of healing

Spiritual power of healing: opening and receptivity to the divine influence.

The Mother, 15: 168

Material power to heal

The material power to heal demands a great sincerity in one's goodwill.

The Mother, 15: 168

The Healer

Nature is the all-round Healer.

The Mother, 15: 172

A force working

... it is possible for the doctor to have felt a force working in him and guiding him or he may see the patient improving with a rapidity which, according to medical science, is incredible.

Sri Aurobindo 22: 217

Successful doctors

On the contrary if one develops the diagnostic flair one can see at once what is the real thing among the possibilities and see what is to be done. That is what the most successful doctors have, they have the flashlight which shows them the true point.

Sri Aurobindo, 25: 377

Healing capacity

To medical knowledge and experience, add full faith in the Divine's Grace and your healing capacity will have no limits.

The Mother, 15: 167

Reliance on the Divine

There is no harm in a doctor who is a sadhak carrying on his profession and using his medical knowledge; but he should do it in reliance on the Divine Grace and the Divine Will; if he can get true inspiration to aid his science, so much the better. No doctor can cure all cases. You are to do your best with the best result you can.

Sri Aurobindo, 24: 1568-69

What the doctor says

But as a general rule I feel that when one goes to a doctor for treatment, one should do what he says....

Our help and our blessings are always with you, affectionately.

The Mother, 17: 192

The Ways:
Physical Culture

Role of physical culture

And your body, if you draw from it all the possibilities it holds, if you educate it by the normal, well-known, scientific methods, if you make this instrument into something as perfect as possible, then, when the supramental truth manifests in that body, it will become *immediately* – without centuries of preparation – a marvellous instrument for the expression of the Spirit.

The Mother, 9: 94

Physical education at any age

But if for any reason this physical education has not been given during childhood or even in youth, it can begin at any age and be pursued throughout life.

The Mother, 12: 27

Assure the child good health

In the general programme of the child's education, sports and outdoor games should be given a prominent place; that, more than all medicines in the world, will assure the child good health.

The Mother, 12: 15

Eat in order to ...

From one's very childhood, one should know that one eats in order to give strength and health to the body and not to enjoy the pleasures of the palate.

The Mother, 12: 14

Desires and needs

... one must educate the child with care and teach him to distinguish his desires from his needs.

The Mother, 12: 13

Cleanliness and hygienic habits

Another thing should be taught to a child from his early years: to enjoy cleanliness and observe hygienic habits. But, in obtaining this cleanliness and respect for the rules of hygiene from the child, one must take care not to instil into him the fear of illness.

The Mother, 12: 14

Education of the body

All education of the body should begin at birth and continue throughout life. It is never too soon to begin nor too late to continue.

The Mother, 12: 12

Undergo a rigorous discipline of the body

One must already be something of a sage to be able to undergo a rigorous discipline of the body and obtain from it the ordered, regular effort which can perfect it. There is no longer any room there for all the fancies of desire. You see, as soon as one gives way to excesses, to immoderation of any kind and a disorderly life, it becomes quite impossible to control one's body and develop it normally, not to mention that, naturally, one spoils one's health and as a result the most important part of the ideal of a perfect body disappears; for with bad health, impaired health, one is not much good for anything. And it is certainly the satisfaction of desires and impulses of the vital or the unreasonable demands of certain ambitions which make the body suffer and fall ill.

The Mother, 9: 99

Man and woman

What roles should man and woman play in our new way of life? What shall be the relation between them?

Why make at all a distinction between them? They are all equally human beings, trying to become fit instruments for the Divine Work, above sex, caste, creed and nationality, all children of the same Infinite Mother and aspirants to the one Eternal Godhead.

The Mother, 12: 298

A most effective help

...to learn to live not like an animal man, but as a human being, candidate for Divinity.

And the first step towards this realisation is to become the master of this body instead of remaining an impotent slave.

One most effective help towards this goal is physical culture.

The Mother, 12: 294

Importance of physical education

We must not hesitate to give a primary importance to this physical education whose very purpose is to make our body capable of receiving and expressing the new force which seeks to manifest upon earth.

The Mother, 12: 294

Make the body strong and supple

...by means of a rational and discerning physical education, we must make our body strong and supple

enough to become a fit instrument in the material world
for the truth-force which wants to manifest through us.

The Mother, 12: 7

Respect health

Nowadays a well-built, robust, muscular, strong and
well-balanced body is appreciated at its true value. In
this case, children should be taught to respect health
and admire the healthy man whose vigorous body
knows how to repel attacks of illness.

The Mother, 12: 14

The body's capacities

The body has a wonderful capacity of adaptation and
endurance. It is able to do so many more things than
one usually imagines. If, instead of the ignorant and
despotic masters that now govern it, it is ruled by the
central truth of the being, you will be amazed at what it
is capable of doing.

The Mother, 12: 7

Combination of all exercises

Physical education means chiefly the combination of
all exercises for the sake of the growth and upkeep of
the body.

The Mother, 12: 290

Physical science

These ordinary physical means make up the whole science which has accumulated through thousands of years of human existence. This science is very complex, its processes innumerable, complicated, uncertain, often contradictory, always progressive and almost absolutely relative! Still, very precise results have been achieved; ever since physical culture has become a serious preoccupation, a certain number of experiments, studies, observations have accumulated, which enable us to regulate diet, activities, exercise, the whole outer organisation of life, and provide an adequate basis so that those who make the effort to study and conform strictly to these things have a chance to maintain their body in good health, correct the defects it may have and improve its general condition and even achieve results which are sometimes quite remarkable.

The Mother, 9: 109

Consciousness in the body

Physical culture is the best way of developing the consciousness of the body, and the more the body is conscious, the more it is capable of receiving the divine forces that are at work to transform it and give birth to the new race.

The Mother, 12: 285

Physical education

Physical Education is meant to bring into the body, consciousness and control, discipline and mastery, all things necessary for a higher and better life.

The Mother, 12: 276

A solid base

We want to come in contact with the supreme consciousness, the universal consciousness, we want to bring it down in ourselves and to manifest it. But for that we must have a very solid base; our base is our physical being, our body. Therefore we have to build up a body solid, healthy, enduring, skilful, agile and strong, ready for everything. There is no better way to prepare the body than physical exercise: sports, athletics, gymnastics, and all games are the best means to develop and strengthen the body.

The Mother, 12: 278

Way to physical transformation

The world is preparing for a new creation, let us help through physical education, by making our bodies stronger, more receptive and more plastic, on the way to physical transformation.

The Mother, 12: 280

For boys and for girls

In all cases, as well for boys as for girls, the exercises must be graded according to the strength and the capacity of each one. If a weak student tries at once to do hard and heavy exercises, he may suffer for his foolishness. But with a wise and progressive training, girls as well as boys can participate in all kinds of sports, and thus increase their strength and health.

To become strong and healthy can never bring harm to a body, even if it is a woman's body!

The Mother, 12: 296

Teaching the cells to be conscious

Mankind, nearly all of mankind, is conscious only of the physical being. With education, the number of men who are conscious of their vital and mind is increasing. As for the human beings who are conscious of their psychic being, they are relatively few.

If you mean, "How does one awaken the consciousness of the physical being?", that is precisely the aim of physical education. It is physical education that teaches the cells to be conscious.

The Mother, 12: 346-47

What is the body consciousness?

What is the body consciousness? The vital consciousness, of course – the physical consciousness as a whole.

But then, in this physical consciousness as a whole, there is the physical mind – a mind that is occupied with all the ordinary things and responds to everything around you. There is also the vital consciousness, which is the awareness of sensations, impulses, enthusiasms and desires. Finally, there is the physical consciousness it-self, the material consciousness, the body consciousness, and that is the one which has so far never been entirely transformed. The global, overall consciousness of the body has been transformed, that is, one can throw off the bondage of thought, of habits that one no longer considers inevitable. That can change, it has been changed. But what remains to be changed is the con-sciousness of the cells.

The Mother, 15: 315

Consciousness in the cells

There is a consciousness in the cells: it is what we call the "body consciousness" and it is wholly bound up with the body. This consciousness has much diffi-culty in changing, because it is under the influence of the collective suggestion which is absolutely opposed to the transformation. So one has to struggle with this collective suggestion, not only with the collective sug-gestion of the present, but with the collective sugges-tion which belongs to the earth-consciousness as a whole, the terrestrial human consciousness which goes back to the earliest formation of man. That has to be overcome before the cells can be spontaneously aware of the Truth, of the Eternity of matter.

The Mother, 15: 315

Unknown treasures

In the body there are invaluable and unknown treasures. In all its cells, there is an intensity of life, of aspiration, of the will to progress which one does not usually even realise. The body-consciousness would have to be completely warped by the action of the mind and vital for it not to have an immediate will to re-establish the equilibrium. When this will is not there, it means that the entire body-consciousness has been spoilt by the intervention of the mind and vital. In people who cherish their malady more or less subconsciously with a sort of morbidity under the pretext that it makes them interesting, it is not their body at all – poor body! – it is something they have imposed upon it with a mental or vital perversion. The body, if left to itself, is remarkable, for, not only does it aspire for equilibrium and well-being but it is capable of restoring the balance. If one leaves one's body alone without intervening with all those thoughts, all the vital reactions, all the depressions, and also all the so-called knowledge and mental constructions and fears – if one leaves the body to itself, spontaneously it will do what is necessary to set itself right again.

The Mother, 6: 140

Simple heart and mind

It is quite obvious that one of the most powerful means for acting on the body is faith. People who have a simple heart, not a very complicated mind – simple people, you see – who don't have a very great, very complicated mental development but have a very deep faith, have a great power of action over their bodies, very great.

The Mother, 9: 125

March Past

That, the March Past, it is... it is more a physical action— preparing oneself for the physical action. It is more a way of opening oneself to the energy, the universal energy, to prepare for the action. It is a contact with the energy, the universal energy which is there, it is to help the body to participate in the work. At that moment it is something very physical. This is truly the basis of physical culture: to prepare the body for the action and the receptivity of energies to accomplish the work. And also the Marching, even when I am not there. But the March Past is for stimulating the receptivity of the body to the energies for realisation. It is based upon something which is expressed in all kinds of ways; but it is a kind of admiration... how to put it?... a spontaneous and also charming admiration for heroism, which is in the most material physical consciousness.

The Mother, 7: 259

The Ways:
Hatha Yoga

Well-planned exercises

From our experience we have found that a particular
system of exercises cannot be stamped as the only yogic
type of exercises and we cannot definitely say that par-
ticipation in those exercises only will help to gain health
because they are yogic exercises.

Any rational system of exercises suited to one's need
and capacity will help the participant to improve in
health. Moreover it is the attitude that is more important. Any well-planned and scientifically arranged programme of exercises practised with a yogic attitude will
become yogic exercises and the person practising them
will draw full benefit from the point of view of physical
health and moral and spiritual uplift.

The Mother, 12: 287

Action of the conscious will

> *Mother, in the physical education we practise here our aim is a greater and greater control over the body, isn't it? So, as Sri Aurobindo has said in what we read last time, that the Hatha-yoga and Tantric methods give a very great control over the body, why don't we introduce these methods into our system?*

...The basis of all these methods is the power exercised by the conscious will over matter. Usually it is a method which someone has used fairly successfully and set up as a principle of action, which he has taught to others who in turn have continued and perfected it until it has taken a somewhat fixed form of one kind of discipline or another. But the whole basis is the action of the conscious will on the body. The exact form of the method is not of primary importance.

The Mother, 9: 152-53

Conscious movements

The yogi or aspiring yogi who does *asanas* to obtain a spiritual result or even simply a control over his body, obtains these results because it is with this aim that he does them, whereas I know some people who do exactly the same things but for all sorts of reasons unrelated to spiritual development, and who haven't even managed to acquire good health by it! And yet they do exactly the same thing, sometimes they even do it much better than the yogi, but it doesn't give them a stable health...because they haven't thought about it, haven't done it with this purpose in mind. I have asked them myself, I said, "But how can you be ill after doing all that?" – "Oh! but I never thought of it, that's not why I do it." This amounts to saying that it is the conscious will which acts on matter, not the material fact.

But you only have to try it; you will understand very well what I mean. For instance, all the movements you make when dressing, taking your bath, tidying your room... no matter what; make them consciously, with the will that this muscle should work, that muscle should work. You will see, you will obtain really amazing results.

The Mother, 9: 154-55

Going up and down the stairs

Going up and down the stairs – you cannot imagine how useful that can be from the point of view of physical culture, if you know how to make use of it. Instead of going up because you are going up and coming down because you are coming down, like any ordinary man, you go up with the consciousness of all the muscles which are working and of making them work harmoniously. You will see. Just try a little, you will see! This means that you can use all the movements of your life for a harmonious development of your body.

The Mother, 9: 155

Pranayama and health

In Hatha Yoga you are all right so long as you continue the practice. As soon as you leave it off you are liable to attacks.

In Raja Yoga also you have to continue Pranayama once you begin it. My own experience is that when I was practising Pranayam at Baroda, I had excellent health. But when I went to Bengal and left Pranayama, I was attacked by all sorts of illnesses which nearly carried me off.

Sri Aurobindo
[*From "Evening Talks with Sri Aurobindo", recorded by A.B. Purani, p. 518*]

Asana

The first object of the Asana is to conquer the body, for the body must be conquered before it can become divine — to be able to lay any command upon it and never be commanded by it.

Sri Aurobindo, 3: 403

The Ways:
Sleep

Before sleep

Before trying to sleep, when you lie down to sleep, begin by relaxing yourself physically (I call this becoming a rag on the bed).

Then with all the sincerity at your disposal, offer yourself to the Divine in a complete relaxation, and that's all.

The Mother, 15: 143

Tiredness and sleep

But one thing is very important: never go to sleep when you are very tired, for if you do, you fall into a sort of unconsciousness and dreams do with you whatever they like, without your being able to exercise the least control. Just as you should always rest before eating, I would advise you all to rest before going to sleep. But then you must know how to rest.

There are many ways of doing it. Here is one: first of all, put your body at ease, comfortably stretched out on a bed or an easy-chair. Then try to relax your nerves, all together or one by one, till you have obtained complete relaxation. This done, and while your body lies limp like a rag on the bed, make your brain silent and immobile, till it is no longer conscious of itself. Then slowly, imperceptibly, pass from this state into sleep. When you wake up the next morning, you will be full of energy.

The Mother, 15: 142

Physical discipline

I want you to be perfectly healthy. For that, you must follow a physical discipline: sleep regularly, eat regularly, exercise regularly, etc., etc.

The Mother, 16: 127

Take enough rest

I advise you to sleep well and to take enough rest. This is indispensable in order to be able to keep doing the work regularly and well.

The Mother, 15: 141

Insomnia

The only cure for insomnia is to get rid of the need for sleep by knowing how to obtain mental silence at will.

The Mother, 17: 354

Sleep

Sleep is indispensable in the present state of the body. It is by a progressive control over the subconscient that the sleep can become more and more conscious.

The Mother, 15: 141

Quiet sleep

It is in good, sound and quiet sleep that one can get in contact with a deeper part of oneself.

The Mother, 15: 141

The austerity of sleep

It does not consist in going without sleep but in knowing how to sleep. Sleep must not be a fall into unconsciousness which makes the body heavy instead of refreshing. Eating with moderation and abstaining from all excess greatly reduces the need to spend many hours in sleep; however, the quality of sleep is much more important than its quantity. In order to have a truly effective rest and relaxation during sleep, it is good as a rule to drink something before going to bed, a cup of milk or soup or fruit-juice, for instance. Light food brings a quiet sleep.... If before retiring to bed one has talked a lot or had a lively discussion, if one has read an exciting or intensely interesting book, one should rest a little without sleeping in order to quieten the mental activity, so that the brain does not engage in disorderly movements while the other parts of the body alone are asleep.

The Mother, 12: 52

Before falling asleep

To begin with, when one is conscious of one's nights, the first thing to do before falling fast asleep, just in the state when one begins to relax, relax all one's nerves – I have explained this to you already, one relaxes all the nerves and lets oneself go... like this... you know – well, at that moment, one must relax very carefully all mental activity and make that quiet, as quiet as possible, and not go off to sleep until the mind is quite calm.

The Mother, 6: 185

Extremely conscious

But there is the possibility of a sleep in which you enter into an absolute silence, immobility and peace in all parts of your being and your consciousness merges into Sachchidananda. You can hardly call it sleep, for it is extremely conscious. In that condition you may remain for a few minutes, but these few minutes give you more rest and refreshment than hours of ordinary sleep. You cannot have it by chance; it requires a long training.

The Mother, 3: 16

The Ways:
Food

Food

The all-absorbing interest which nearly all human beings even the most intellectual, have in food, its preparation and its consumption, should be replaced by an almost chemical knowledge of the needs of the body and a very scientific austerity in satisfying them.

The Mother, 12: 52

Eating depends on the state of your health

Will You please give me directions about food?

What you should eat depends on the general state of your health, on what is lacking in your body and on what it cannot tolerate. This only a doctor who is an expert on the subject can say.

The food should be very clean, very healthy and strengthening. Moral restrictions are inventions of the

human mind and ought to be disregarded when necessary.

Food should be taken exclusively according to the
needs of the body and not according to rules, conven-
tions and desires.

The Mother,   Bulletin, April 2005, p. 19

A prayer

O divine Light, supramental Reality:

With this food, penetrate the whole body, enter into
every cell, establish Thyself in every atom; may everything become perfectly sincere and receptive, free from
all that obstructs the manifestation, in short, open to
Thee all the parts of my body that are not already Thyself.

The Mother, 13: 58

Sacred offering

Our commonest or most grossly material actions must
assume this sublimated character; when we eat, we
should be conscious that we are giving food to that Presence in us; it must be a sacred offering in a temple and
the sense of a mere physical need or self-gratification
must pass away from us.

Sri Aurobindo, 20: 103

Control the food

Unless you control the food you take, you will always be ill.

The Mother, 15: 159

Conquest over greed

Conquest over the greed for food: a promise of good health.

The Mother, 15: 160

Need and greed

A sadhak must eat to satisfy the need of his body not to meet the demand of his greed.

The Mother, 14: 270

Pleasures of the palate

If you prefer the pleasures of the palate to the union with the Divine, it is your own look-out and I have nothing to say, except that I do not approve, but each one must be free to choose whether he will rise above his lower nature or sink down in the material pit.

The Mother, 14: 270

Freedom from attachment

It is an inner attitude of freedom from attachment

and from greed for food and desire of the palate that is needed, not undue diminution of the quantity taken or any self-starvation.

The Mother, 14: 270

Party

> My most beloved Mother, I think it would be better to avoid a party of this kind.

Evidently, this creates an atmosphere in which food predominates; this is not very conducive to spiritual life.

The Mother, 16: 196

Truth of the problem

> Sweet Mother,
> People often say that our food does not contain enough vitamins and protein. The doctors claim that this is why we have so much physical and bodily suffering. Is it really the cause? Does food have such an important place in life?

For those whose consciousness is centered *in the body*, who live for the body, its desires and satisfactions, those for whom the *truth* begins and ends *with the body*, it is evident that food is of capital importance since they *live to eat*.

The doctors are always anxious to throw the responsibility for their incompetence to cure on the external conditions of life.

If one wants to see the truth of the problem, it is this: only an enlightened body, balanced and free from all vital desire and mental preconception, is capable of knowing what it needs in regard to quantity and kind of food – and it is so exceptional to find such a body that we need not speak of it.

Apart from that, one must act for the best and not attach too much importance to it.

Let those who have confidence in doctors do as they advise and see if it helps them to suffer less!

The Mother, 16: 302-03

Attitude to food

Greed for food has to be overcome, but it has not to be given too much thought. The proper attitude to food is a certain equality. Food is for the maintenance of the body and one should take enough for that – what the body needs; if one gives less the body feels the need and hankers; if you give more, then that is indulging the vital.

Sri Aurobindo, 24: 1467

Before you eat

Thus before you eat, concentrate a few seconds in the aspiration that the food you are about to eat may bring your body the substance it needs to serve as a solid basis for your effort towards the great discovery, and give it the energy for persistence and perseverance in the effort.

The Mother, 12: 34

Eat in order to

From one's very childhood, one should know that one eats in order to give strength and health to the body and not to enjoy the pleasures of the palate.

The Mother, 12: 14

Not by abstaining from food

It is not by abstaining from food that you can make a spiritual progress. It is by being free, not only from all attachment and all desire and preoccupation with food, but even from all need for it; by being in the state in which all these things are so foreign to your consciousness that they have no place there. Only then, as a spontaneous, natural result, can one usefully stop eating. It could be said that the essential condition is to forget to eat – forget, because all the energies of the being and all its concentration are turned towards a more total, more true inner realisation, towards this *constant*, imperative preoccupation with the union of the whole being, including the bodily cells, with the vibration of the divine forces, with the supramental force which is manifesting, so that this may be the true life: not only the purpose of life, but the essence of life, not only an imperative need of life, but all its joy and all its *raison d'être*.

The Mother, 9: 117

An equanimity

To conquer the greed for food an equanimity in the
being must be developed such that you are perfectly
indifferent towards food. If food is given you, you eat
it; if not, it does not worry you in the least; above all,
you do not keep thinking about food. And the thinking
must not be negative, either. To be absorbed in devis-
ing methods and means of abstinence as the *sannyasis*
do is to be almost as preoccupied with food as to be
absorbed in dreaming of it greedily. Have an attitude
of indifference towards it: that is the main thing. Get
the idea of food out of your consciousness, do not attach the slightest importance to it.

The Mother, 3: 123

Taking in inconscience

Physically, we depend upon food to live – unfortunately. For with food, we daily and constantly take in a
formidable amount of inconscience, of *tamas*, heaviness,
stupidity. One can't do otherwise – unless constantly,
without a break, we remain completely aware and, as
soon as an element is introduced into our body, we immediately work upon it to extract from it only the light
and reject all that may darken our consciousness. This
is the origin and rational explanation of the religious
practice of consecrating one's food to God before taking it. When eating one aspires that this food may not

be taken for the little human ego but as an offering to the divine consciousness within oneself.

The Mother, 4: 334

Before eating

And then again, even when this has been done, there is still the problem of food; as long as our body is compelled to take in foreign matter in order to subsist, it will absorb at the same time a considerable amount of inert and unconscious forces or those having a rather undesirable consciousness, and this alchemy must take place inside the body. We were speaking of the kinds of consciousness absorbed with food, but there is also the inconscience that's absorbed with food—quite a deal of it. And that is why in many yogas there was the advice to offer to the Divine what one was going to eat before eating it (*Mother makes a gesture of offering, hands joined, palms open*). It consists in calling the Divine down into the food before eating it. One offers it to Him—that is, one puts it in contact with the Divine, so that it may be under the divine influence when one eats it. It is very useful, it is very good.

The Mother, 6: 214

The Ways:
Spiritual Force

Supraphysical Force

> Q: I contented that the healing force will act only
> through The Mother, and others will be able to wield it
> if they are in some way open to or in conscious rapport
> with her and in physical contact with her. Nobody will
> be able to use it without fulfilling these conditions. What
> do you say?

A: At first it will be no doubt like that, if it is to be the
true Force, but when once it is settled in the earth- consciousness, a more general use of the supraphysical
Force for healing may become possible.

Sri Aurobindo, 25: 162

Illness can be repelled

On the other side, there can be an opposite use and
result of the Yogic consciousness: illness can be repelled

from one's own body or cured, even chronic or deep-seated illness and long-established constitutional defects remedied or expelled from one's own body or cured, and even a predestined death delayed for a long period. Narayan Jyotishi, a Calcutta astrologer, who predicted, not knowing then who I was, in the days before my name was politically known, my struggle with Mlechchha enemies and afterwards the three cases against me and my three acquittals, predicted also that though death was prefixed for me in my horoscope at the age of 63, I would prolong my life by Yogic power for a very long period and arrive at a full old age. In fact, I have got rid by Yogic pressure of a number of chronic maladies that had got settled in my body. But none of these instances either on the favorable or unfavorable side can be made into a rule; there is no validity in the tendency of human reason to transform the relativity of these things into an absolute.

Sri Aurobindo, 26: 209

Receptivity to the force

It depends on how far the inner being is awake – otherwise one needs a physical *avalambana*. There are some other people who get the relief only after we read the letter, others get it immediately they write or before it reached us or after it has reached but before we have read. Others get it simply by referring the whole matter to us mentally. Idiosyncracies!

Sri Aurobindo, 26: 500-01

Cancer can be cured

Q: The Mother once said that there is hardly a disease that can not be cured by Yoga. Can cancer be cured by it?

A: Of course it can, but on condition of faith or openness or both. Even a mental suggestion can cure cancer – with luck of course, as is shown by the case of the woman operated on unsuccessfully for cancer, but the doctor lied and told her it had succeeded. Result, cancer symptoms all ceased and she died many years afterwards of another illness altogether.

Sri Aurobindo, 25: 378

The Mother's force

The inherent strength of the body does not do things like that. It is the Mother's force that does it, when one calls and opens oneself…. When you are conscious of the play of the forces, then you feel the working.

It (awakening) means the conscious action of the psychic from behind. When it comes to the front it invades the mind and vital and body and psychicises their movements. It comes best by aspiration and an unquestioning and entire turning and surrender to the Mother. But also it sometimes comes of itself when the *ādhāra* is ready.

Sri Aurobindo, 25: 353

Concentrate

> *Mother,*
> *Will any doctor believe that yesterday when I was*
> *writing my letter to you the swelling of my groin was*
> *so big that I had difficulty in walking. This morning*
> *when you received my letter, I began to feel that it was*
> *shrinking. By the time I got your reply it was reduced*
> *to half. Now I can run! The swelling of the foot also*
> *goes down in the same way, but neither goes away*
> *completely. They reach a point where they are harmless*
> *and then the progress stops.*

This gives the exact measure of your body's receptivity. Concentrate the force on the diseased parts and
they will improve.

The Mother, 17: 296

Receptivity is needed

I mean a certain receptivity in the consciousness –
mind, vital, physical, whichever is needed. The Mother
or myself send a force. If there is no openness, the force
may be thrown back or return (unless we put a great
force which is not advisable to do) as from an obstruc-
tion or resistance: if there is some openness, the result
may be partial or slow; if there is the full openness or
receptivity, then the result may be immediate. Of course,
there are things that cannot be removed all at once, being an old part of the nature, but with receptivity these

also can be more effectively and rapidly dealt with. Some people are so open that even by writing they get free before the book or letter reaches us.

Sri Aurobindo, 26: 500

Working of the force through allopaths and homeopaths

The Mother and I have no preference for allopathy. The Mother thinks doctors very usually make things worse instead of better by spoiling Nature's resistance to illness by excessive and ill-directed use of their medicines. We have been able to work through X's homeopathy far better than through anything else – though it is likely that the Force working through homeopaths, who were not conscious instruments, might not have succeeded better than with the allopaths.

Sri Aurobindo, 26: 501

It is like that

> *Mother, I am asking you a small personal question. An incurable illness, an organic disease has been cured by your grace, but a purely functional illness is not. How can that be? In the same body. Is it a lack of receptivity or...?*

It is something so personal, so individual, that it is impossible to reply. As I said, for each one the case is absolutely different, and one can't give an explanation for these things without going into the details of the functioning. For each one, the case is different....

Indeed, when one sees this in its totality and its essence, the wisest thing one can say is: "It is like that because it is like that."

The Mother, 9: 126

Constantly at work

In the whole manifestation there is an infinite Grace constantly at work to bring the world out of the misery, the obscurity and the stupidity in which it lies. From all time this Grace has been at work, unremitting in its effort, and how many thousands of years were necessary for this world to awaken to the need for something greater, more true, more beautiful.

The Mother, 9: 420

The Secret

A single thought turned towards Thee

O Lord, Master of our life, let us soar very high above all care for our material preservation. Nothing is more humiliating and depressing than these thoughts so constantly turned towards the preservation of the body, these preoccupations with health, the means of subsistence, the framework of life.... How very insignificant is all this, a thin smoke that a simple breath can disperse or a single thought turned towards Thee dispel like a vain mirage!

The Mother, 1: 30

Teaching the body

As many cases
so many cures.

The most important thing in therapeutics is to teach the body to react properly and reject the illness.

The Mother, 15: 171

The mystic voyage

And never can the mystic voyage cease,
Till the nescient dusk is lifted from man's soul
And the morns of God have overtaken his night.

Sri Aurobindo, 28: 72

The imperative condition

The imperative condition for cure is calm and quietness. Any agitation, any narrowness prolongs the illness.

The Mother, 15: 163

Pushing peace into the cells

Catch hold of a peace deep within and push it into the cells of the body. With the peace will come back the health.

The Mother, 15: 163

The secret remedy

Peace and stillness are the great remedy for disease. When we can bring peace in our cells, we are cured.

The Mother, 15: 163

Peace in the nerves

Peace in the nerves: indispensable for good health.

The Mother, 15: 163

Purity

Purity in the cells cannot be obtained except through conquest of desire; it is the true condition for good health.

The Mother, 14: 384

Keep quiet

To keep quiet and to concentrate, leaving the Force from above to do its work, is the surest way to be cured of anything and everything.

The Mother, 15: 160

Keep a peaceful faith

You must not lose patience, this does not hasten the cure. On the contrary, you must keep a peaceful faith that you are going to be cured.

The Mother, 15: 160

This is the cure

Turn your mind completely away from your difficulty, concentrate exclusively on the Light and the Force coming from above; let the Lord do for your body whatever He pleases. Hand over to Him totally the entire responsibility of your physical being.

This is the cure.

The Mother, 15: 162

The figure 100

The figure 100 in itself has no special significance for the length of a human life. But simply because human life has become so complex, it has also become relatively short, and it is now rare to live to be a hundred.

When man lived in harmony with Nature, his life lasted longer.

When man lives by and for the Divine, his life will be longer, and one day the Divine will reveal to him the secret of immortality.

The Mother, 17: 378

Will to conquer illness

Wake up in yourself a will to conquer. Not a mere will in the mind but a will in the very cells of your body. Without that you can't do anything; you may take a hundred medicines but they won't cure you unless you have a will to overcome the physical illness.

The Mother, 15: 158

Put a strong will

You must put a strong will for getting rid of your illness and you must remain quiet and unperturbed by the results.

The Mother, 15: 158

Illness – an opportunity

Your illness gave you an opportunity to open your eyes towards the need for an inner change. You must take advantage of this and progress.

The Mother, 15: 150

Only to the divine influence

It is good to do exercises and to lead a simple and hygienic life, but for the body to be truly perfect, it must open to the divine forces, it must be subject only to the divine influence, it must aspire constantly to realise the Divine.

The Mother, 15: 147

Equality

Physical troubles always come as lessons to teach *equality* and to reveal what in us is pure and luminous enough to remain unaffected. It is in equality that one finds the remedy.

The Mother, 15: 149

Illness – a test

The illness has come like a test and gone like a puri- fication carrying away all that was standing in the way of the joy of an integral consecration.

The Mother, 15: 149

Cure

The body is cured if it has decided to be cured.

The Mother, 15: 159

Reject illness

The body should reject illness as energetically as we reject falsehood in the mind.

The Mother, 15: 159

The spirit within

The spirit within us is the only all-efficient doctor and submission of the body to it the one true panacea.

Sri Aurobindo, 17: 127

God within

God within is infinite and self-fulfilling Will. Unaffected by the fear of death canst thou leave to Him, not as an experiment, but with a calm and entire faith thy ailments? Thou shalt find that in the end He exceeds the skill of a million doctors.

Sri Aurobindo, 17: 127

Seek to discover

Surgeons save and cure by cutting and maiming. Why not rather seek to discover Nature's direct all-powerful remedies?

Sri Aurobindo, 17: 128

Open to the Force

As the body consciousness becomes more open to the Force (it is always the most difficult and the last to open up entirely), this frequent stress of illness will diminish and disappear.

Sri Aurobindo, 24: 1567

Go deep within

This delight, this wonderful laughter that dissolves every shadow, every pain, every suffering! You only have to go deep enough within yourself to find the inner Sun, to let yourself be flooded by it; and then there is nothing but a cascade of harmonious, luminous, sunlit laughter, which leaves no room for any shadow or pain.

The Mother, 10: 158

Be regular in your material life

Only when you become absolutely regular in your material life will you be able to have good health.

The Mother, 16: 132

Certitude of cure

The body carries within itself the certitude of cure, the certitude that the illness or disorder is sure to disappear. It is only through the false education from the environment that gradually the body is taught that there are incurable diseases, irreparable accidents, and that it can grow old, and all these stories which destroy its faith and trust. But normally, the body of a normal child – the body, I am not speaking of the thought – the body itself feels when something goes wrong that it will certainly be all right again. And if it is not like that, this means that it has already been perverted. It seems *normal* for it to be in good health, it seems quite abnormal to it if something goes wrong and it falls ill; and in its instinct, its spontaneous instinct, it is sure that everything will be all right. It is only the perversion of thought which destroys this; as one grows up the thought becomes more and more distorted, there is the whole collective suggestion, and so, little by little, the body loses its trust in itself, and naturally, losing its self-confidence, it also loses the spontaneous capacity of restoring its equilibrium when this has been disturbed.

The Mother, 9: 163

Immune to every attack

> *Sweet Mother, how can we make the body immune to every attack?*

...He [Sri Aurobindo] says that only the descent of the supramental Force can make the body immune to every attack. He says that otherwise it is only momentary, and that it doesn't always work. He says that it can be practically immune but not absolutely so; and to be absolutely so, it is only by transforming the nature as it is into a supramental nature that one can make the body absolutely immune to all attacks.

The Mother, 7: 143

Body – a creature of habits

To change one's body one must be ready to do millions of times the same thing, because the body is a creature of habits and functions by routine, and because to destroy a routine one must persevere for years.

The Mother, 7: 105

Union with the divine forces

We are at a moment of transition in the history of the earth. It is merely a moment in eternal time, but this moment is long compared to human life. Matter is changing in order to prepare itself for the new manifestation, but the human body is not plastic enough and offers resistance; this is why the number of incomprehensible disorders and even diseases is increasing and becoming a problem for medical science.

The remedy lies in union with the divine forces that are at work and a receptivity full of trust and peace which makes the task easier.

The Mother, 16: 421

Mastering physical suffering

How to master physical suffering?

I might say: the cells of the body must learn to seek their support only in the Divine, until the moment when they are able to feel that they are the expression of the Divine.

The Mother, 11: 273

Do not worry

> *Sweet Mother,*
> *I ardently pray to You to pull me out of this condition of bad health and make me progress integrally. You know that my soul's only aspiration is to love You and serve You. Make me physically active in Your service.*

You have been and still remain a faithful servitor. Do not worry: if your body is no longer fit for physical work, take advantage of all the time at your disposal to develop your inner consciousness and unite more and more consciously with the Divine.

Reading, meditation, contemplation, self-giving, in silence and concentration, to the Divine who is always present to hear you and guide you.

The Mother, 17: 355

Complete immunity

Absolute cure of an illness so that it cannot return again depends on clearing the mind, the vital and body consciousness of the psychological response to the Force bringing the illness.... The complete immunity from all illness for which our yoga tries can only come by a total and permanent enlightenment of the below from above resulting in the removal of the psychological roots of ill health – it can't be done otherwise.

Sri Aurobindo, 24: 1571

Call in the Mother's Force

You must not accept but reject it with your physical mind and so help the body consciousness to throw off the suggestion. If necessary, make a counter-suggestion "No, I shall be well; I am and shall be all right." And in any case call in the Mother's Force to throw out the suggestion and the illness it is bringing.

Sri Aurobindo, 24: 1572

The most powerful help

All illnesses are obviously due to the imperfect nature of the body and the physical nature. The body can be immune only when it is open to the higher consciousness and the latter can descend into it. Till then what he writes is the remedy – if he can also call in the force to throw out the illness that is the most powerful help possible.

Sri Aurobindo, 24: 1563

Slight touch of the Force

If the subconscient also answers, then even a slight touch of the Force can not only cure the particular illness but make that form and kind of illness practically impossible hereafter.

Sri Aurobindo, 24: 1570

Leaving to Him the responsibility

…the best way to be healthy is to concentrate all our consciousness on the Divine, leaving to Him the responsibility of taking care of our body. Then we have only to be attentive to the orders that He gives us in all circumstances, and obey them scrupulously.

The Mother, Bulletin, April 2005

Invoke the Divine Presence

I know by experience that one can stop a tooth-ache in a few minutes if the *spot that is suffering* invokes the Divine Presence in a total surrender.

But if you have not yet learned to do this in the body, not mentally, it is better to go to Dr. X who will treat you.

The Mother, Bulletin, April 2005, p. 35

If one knows how to surrender

When physical conditions are a little difficult and some discomfort follows, if one knows how to surrender completely before Thy will, caring little for life or death, health or illness, the integral being enters immediately into harmony with Thy law of love and life, and

all physical indisposition ceases giving place to a calm
well-being, deep and peaceful.

The Mother, 1: 101

Body's essence is divine

The body must know and be convinced that its essence
is divine and that if no obstacle is put in the way of the
Divine's working, nothing can harm us. This process
must be steadily repeated until all recurrence of fear is
stopped. And then even if the illness succeeds in making
its appearance, its strength and duration will be consid-
erably diminished until it is definitively conquered.

The Mother, 14: 151

Faith

Have faith. There is no disease which cannot be cured
by the Divine Grace.

The Mother, 15: 164

Grace

Do not think you are invalid for ever, because the
Grace of the Lord is infinite.

The Mother, 15: 164

Turn towards the Divine

Turn towards the Divine, all your sufferings will disappear.

The Mother, 14: 266

Throw away fear

The real disease is fear. Throw the fear away and the disease will go.

The Mother, 15: 152

Two essential things

If you want to get cured there are two conditions. First you must be without fear, absolutely fearless, you understand, and secondly you must have a complete faith in the Divine protection. These two things are essential.

The Mother, 15: 152

Absolute faith

One could say in conclusion that it is the faith of the patient which gives the remedy its power to heal.

If men had an absolute faith in the healing power of Grace, they would perhaps avoid many illnesses.

The Mother, 10: 325

Not to forget

If you are ill, your illness is looked after with so much anxiety and fear, you are given so much care that you forget to take help from the One who can help you and you fall into a vicious circle and take a morbid interest in your illness.

The Mother, 15: 155

Surrender to the Divine's Will

Physical ailments are always the sign of a resistance in the physical being; but with surrender to the Divine's Will and a complete trust in the working of the Grace, they are bound to disappear soon.

The Mother, 15: 148

Faith in the doctor and the medicine

It is not the medicine that cures so much as the patient's faith in the doctor and the medicine. Both are a clumsy substitute for the natural faith in one's own self-power which they have themselves destroyed.

Sri Aurobindo, 17: 126

Never lose hope or faith

One must never lose hope or faith – there is nothing incurable, and no limit can be set to the power of the Divine.

The Mother, 16: 195

Conquest of desire

Purity in the cells cannot be obtained except through conquest of desire; it is the true condition for good health.

The Mother, 14: 384

Concentrate with affection and good will

If you know how to think correctly, with force and intelligence and kindness, if you love someone and wish him well very sincerely, deeply, with all your heart, that does him much good, much more certainly than you think. I have said this often; for example, to those who are here, who learn that someone in their family is very ill and feel that childish impulse of wanting to rush immediately to the spot to attend to the sick person. I tell you, unless it is an exceptional case and there is nobody to attend on the sick person (and at times even in such a case), if you know how to keep the right attitude and concentrate with affection and good will upon the sick person, if you know how to pray for him and make helpful formations, you will do him much more good than if you go to nurse him, feed him, help him wash himself, indeed all that everybody can do. Anybody can nurse a person. But not everybody can make good formations and send out forces that act for healing.

The Mother, 5: 133-34

Bring down peace

> Mother,
> I have been rather unwell for the last three or four days,
> diarrhea and vomiting are the symptoms. Generally
> this happens when my mind is upset, but this time it is
> not so. I did not eat for three days and I was all right.
> Yesterday I took some food and again the problem has
> started. The real reason must be somewhere else?

It is due to restlessness and agitation. What is the matter?

Bring down peace, the *Divine Peace* in your stomach and it will be all right.

Love and blessings

The Mother, 17: 315-16

Reducing the illness

Some people are spontaneously free from fear even in their body; they have a sufficient vital equilibrium in them not to be afraid, not to fear, and a natural harmony in the rhythm of their physical life which enables them to reduce the illness spontaneously to a minimum.

The Mother, 9: 122

The only true remedy

We cannot counteract the harm done by mental faith in the need for drugs by any external measures. Only by escaping from the mental prison and emerging consciously into the light of the spirit, by a conscious union with the Divine, can we enable Him to give back to us the balance and health we have lost.

The supramental transformation is the only true remedy.

The Mother, 10: 327

Excellent health

A perfect harmony in the proportions, suppleness and strength, grace and force, plasticity and endurance, and above all, an excellent health, unvarying and unchanging, which is the result of a pure soul, a happy trust in life and an unshakable faith in the Divine Grace.

The Mother, 12: 298

The imperative condition

The imperative condition for cure is calm and quietness. Any agitation, any narrowness prolongs the illness.

The Mother, 15: 163

The psychic contact

This peace and fullness and joy given by the psychic contact they naturally find everywhere, in everything and everybody. It gives an openness towards the true consciousness pervading here and working out everything. So long as the openness is there, the peace, the fullness and the joy remain with their immediate results of progress, health and fitness in the physical, quietness and goodwill in the vital, clear understanding and broadness in the mental and a general feeling of security and satisfaction. But it is difficult for a human being to keep up a constant contact with his psychic.

The Mother, 12: 45

There would be no illness

If the whole being could simultaneously advance in its progressive transformation, keeping pace with the inner march of the universe, there would be no illness, there would be no death.

The Mother, 3: 90

Each cell is a world

The cells have an inner composition or structure which corresponds to the structure of the universe. So the link is established between identical external and internal states.... It is not "external", but it is external for the individual. That is, the cell, in its internal composition, receives the vibration of the corresponding state in the composition of the whole. Each cell is composed of different radiances, with a wholly luminous centre, and the connection is established between light and light. That is, the will, the central light, acts on the cell by touching the corresponding lights, by an inner contact of the being. Each cell is a world in miniature corresponding to the whole.

The Mother, 12: 345-46

Transformation of the body

Is the will for progress enough to prevent the deterioration that comes with time? How can the physical being prevent this deterioration?

That is precisely what the transformation of the body is: the physical cells not only become conscious, but receptive to the true Consciousness-Force; that is, they allow the working of this higher Consciousness. That is the work of transformation.

The Mother, 12: 346

Absolute sincerity

These congenital diseases can be cured only by an integral transformation of the body itself and we have not reached yet that period in the sadhana; otherwise it is only a so-called "miraculous cure" that can take place and that kind of "miracle" can happen only as the result of an absolute sincerity in the consecration to the Divine and an unshakable faith in the Divine Grace.

The Mother, 15: 164

Opportunity

Indeed, what better use could one make of an illness than to take the opportunity to go deep within oneself and awaken, take birth into a new consciousness, more luminous and more true.

Our help and our blessings are always with you, affectionately.

The Mother, 17: 193

Inner and outer calm

To relieve tension, ten minutes of *real calm*, inner and outer, are more effective than all the remedies in the world. In silence lies the most effective help.

The Mother, 17: 195

True faith

Have the faith, the true faith, that you will be cured and the cure is bound to come.

The Mother, 15: 161

Only the Divine

Only the Divine can heal. It is in *Him alone* that one must seek help and support, it is in *Him alone* that one must put all one's hope.

The Mother, 16: 185

Let Thy Will be done

Instead of being upset and struggling, the best thing to do is to offer one's body to the Divine with the *sincere prayer*, "Let Thy Will be done." If there is any possibility of cure, it will establish the best conditions for it;

and if cure is impossible, it will be the very best preparation for getting out of the body and the life without it.

In any case the first indispensable condition is a quiet surrender to the Divine's will.

The Mother, 15: 161

Faith in the Divine Grace

All the circumstances of life are arranged to teach us that, beyond mind, faith in the Divine Grace gives us the strength to go through all trials, to overcome all weaknesses and find the contact with the Divine Consciousness which gives us not only peace and joy but also physical balance and good health.

The Mother, 10: 323

Faith

Finally it is Faith that cures.

The Mother, 15: 172

Leave it to the Divine

Health: not to be preoccupied with it, but to leave it to the Divine.

The Mother, 15: 154

Q: What can one do against obsession when there is very intense suffering?

A: Look at a beautiful flower.

The Mother, 17: 104

The Secret of Pain & Suffering

Hammer of the gods

Pain is the hammer of the gods to break
A dead resistance in the mortal's heart,
His slow inertia as of living stone.

Sri Aurobindo, 29: 443

Hand of Nature

Pain is the hand of Nature sculpturing men
To greatness: an inspired labour chisels
With heavenly cruelty an unwilling mould.

Sri Aurobindo, 29: 444

Signature of the Ignorance

Pain is the signature of the Ignorance
Attesting the secret god denied by life:
Until life finds him pain can never end.

Sr Aurobindo, 29: 453

Author of thy pain

O mortal who complainst of death and fate,
Accuse none of the harms thyself hast called;
This troubled world thou hast chosen for thy home,
Thou art thyself the author of thy pain.

Sri Aurobindo, 29: 454

Bliss

Bliss is the secret stuff of all that lives,
Even pain and grief are garbs of world-delight,
It hides behind thy sorrow and thy cry.

Sri Aurobindo, 29: 454

Suffering

*Mother, is there really any suffering in our yoga?
When people suffer, are they suffering because of the
difficulties?*

No. Usually they suffer because of a lack of sincerity.

Perhaps they are seeking satisfaction through suffering!

Yes, that also happens.

I think all suffering in this yoga is imaginary.

Yes...

We suffer through our own stupidity.

Usually, it is so.

The Mother, 17: 149

Suffering is not indispensable

Certainly the suffering is not indispensable, nor even necessary. It is indeed ignorance that makes one suffer.

The Mother, 17: 129

Pain due to limitation

Pain is caused because the physical consciousness in the Ignorance is too limited to bear the touches that come upon it. Otherwise, to cosmic consciousness in its state of complete knowledge and complete experience all touches come as Ananda.

Sri Aurobindo, 24: 1579

Pain–the touch of our Mother

Pain is the touch of our Mother teaching us how to bear and grow in rapture. She has three stages of her schooling, endurance first, next equality of soul, last ecstasy.

Sri Aurobindo, 17: 89

Pain and grief

Pain and grief are Nature's reminder to the soul that the pleasure it enjoys is only a feeble hint of the real delight of existence. In each pain and torture of our being is the secret of a flame of rapture compared with which our greatest pleasures are only as dim flickerings. It is this secret which forms the attraction for the soul of the great ordeals, suffering and fierce experiences of life which the nervous mind in us shuns and abhors.

Sri Aurobindo, 16: 386

Pain – first-born of the Inconscience

Pain was the first-born of the Inconscience
Which was thy body's dumb original base;
Already slept there pain's subconscient shape:
A shadow in a shadowy tenebrous womb,
Till life shall move, it waits to wake and be.

Sri Aurobindo, 29: 443

Pain comes to teach us

When pain comes, it comes to teach us something. The quicker we learn it, the more the need for pain diminishes, and when we know the secret, it will no longer be possible to suffer, for that secret reveals to us the reason, the cause, the origin of suffering, and the way to pass beyond it.

The Mother, 9: 41

Overcome suffering

How can suffering be overcome?

The problem is not as simple as all that. The causes of suffering are innumerable and its quality also varies a great deal, although the origin of suffering is one and the same and comes from the initial action of an anti-divine will. To make this easier to understand, one can divide suffering into two distinct categories, although in practice they are very often mixed.

The first is purely egoistic and comes from a feeling that one's rights have been violated, that one has been deprived of one's needs, offended, despoiled, betrayed, injured, etc. This whole category of suffering is clearly the result of hostile action and it not only opens the door in the consciousness to the influence of the adversary but is also one of his most powerful ways of acting in the world, the most powerful of all if in addition there comes its natural and spontaneous consequence: hatred and the desire for revenge in the strong, despair and the wish to die in the weak.

The other category of suffering, whose initial *cause* is the pain of separation created by the adversary, is totally opposite in nature: it is the suffering that comes from divine compassion, the suffering of love that feels compassion for the world's misery, whatever its origin, cause or effect. But this suffering, which is of a purely psychic character, contains no egoism, no self-pity; it is full of peace and strength and power of action, of faith in the future and the will for victory; it does not pity but consoles, it does not identify itself with the ignorant movement in others but cures and illumines it.

It is obvious that in the purity of its essence, only that which is *perfectly divine* can feel that suffering; but partially, momentarily, like flashes of lightning behind the dark clouds of egoism, it appears in all who have a vast and generous heart. However, most often, in the individual consciousness it is mixed with that mean and petty self-pity which is the cause of depression and weakness. Nevertheless, when one is vigilant enough to refuse this mixture or at least to reduce it to a minimum, one soon realises that this divine compassion is based on a sublime and eternal joy which alone has the strength and the power to deliver the world from its ignorance and misery.

And this suffering too will disappear from the universe only with the total disappearance of the adversary and all the effects of his action.

The Mother, 15: 359-60

True faith

Pain brings us back to a deeper truth by obliging us to concentrate in order to be able to bear it, be able to face this thing that crushes us. It is in pain that one most easily finds the true strength again, when one is strong. It is in pain that one most easily finds the true faith again, the faith in something which is above and beyond all pain.

The Mother, 9: 40

Running away from suffering

We must not run away from suffering, we must not love and cultivate it either, we must learn how to go deep down into it sufficiently to turn it into a lever powerful enough for us to force open the doors of the eternal consciousness and enter the serenity of Thy unchanging Oneness.

The Mother, 1: 8

Let all suffering be relieved

Oh! let all tears be wiped away, all suffering relieved, all anguish dispelled, and let calm serenity dwell in every heart and powerful certitude strengthen every mind. Let Thy life flow through all like a regenerating stream that all may turn to Thee and draw from that contemplation the energy for all victories.

The Mother, 1: 49

God's secret

All disease is a means towards some new joy of health, all evil and pain a tuning of Nature for some more intense bliss and good, all death an opening on widest immortality. Why and how this should be so, is God's secret which only the soul purified of egoism can penetrate.

Sri Aurobindo, 17: 94

Seek not after pain

Yet, O soul of man, seek not after pain, for that is not His will, seek after His joy only; as for suffering, it will come to thee surely in His providence as often and as much as is needed for thee. Then bear it that thou mayest find out at last its heart of rapture.

Sri Aurobindo, 17: 141

Pain is the key

Pain is the key that opens the gates of strength; it is the high-road that leads to the city of beatitude.

Sri Aurobindo, 17: 141

Why the pain

Why is thy mind or thy body in pain? Because thy soul behind the veil wishes for the pain or takes delight in it.

Sri Aurobindo, 17: 94

A healthy mind

A healthy mind hates pain; for the desire of pain that men sometimes develop in their minds is morbid and contrary to Nature.

Sri Aurobindo, 17: 144

Balance, calm and peace

… sensibleness is indispensable and the integral yoga is based on balance, calm and peace and not on an unhealthy need to suffer.

The Mother, 14: 48

Pain and Joy

Pain with its lash, joy with its silver bribe
Guard the Wheel's circling immobility.
A bond is put on the high-climbing mind,
A seal on the too large wide-open heart;
Death stays the journeying discoverer, Life.

Sri Aurobindo, 28: 18

The Transition

A tabernacle of God

The body of earth a tabernacle of God.

Sri Aurobindo, 29: 699

The body may reach ...

The supramental consciousness is not a fixed quantity but a power which passes to higher and higher levels of possibility until it reaches supreme consummations of spiritual existence fulfilling supermind and supermind fulfils the ranges of spiritual consciousness that are pushing towards it from the human or mental level. In this progression the body also may reach a more perfect form and a higher range of its expressive powers, become a more and more perfect vessel of divinity.

Sri Aurobindo, 16: 23

Stability of health and strength

Matter after taking into itself and manifesting the power of life and the light of mind would draw down into it the superior or supreme power and light of the spirit and in an earthly body shed its parts of inconscience and become a perfectly conscious frame of the spirit. A secure completeness and stability of the health and strength of its physical tenement could be maintained by the will and force of this inhabitant...

Sri Aurobindo, 16: 18

The spiritualised body

As an instrument the body would acquire a fullness of capacity, a totality of fitness for all uses which the inhabitant would demand of it far beyond anything now possible. Even it could become a revealing vessel of a supreme beauty and bliss, – casting the beauty of the light of the spirit suffusing and radiating from it as a lamp reflects and diffuses the luminosity of its indwelling flame, carrying in itself the beatitude of the spirit, its joy of the seeing mind, its joy of life and spiritual happiness, the joy of Matter released into a spiritual consciousness and thrilled with a constant ecstasy. This would be the total perfection of the spiritualised body.

Sri Aurobindo, 16: 18

Action of the spirit

Even within the limits of its present evolution it is difficult to measure the degree to which the mind is able to extend its control or its use of the body's powers and capacities and when the mind rises to higher powers still and pushes back its human boundaries, it becomes impossible to fix any limits: even, in certain realisations, an intervention by the will in the automatic working of the bodily organs seems to become possible. Wherever limitations recede and in proportion as they recede, the body becomes a more plastic and responsive and in that measure a more fit and perfect instrument of the action of the spirit.

Sri Aurobindo, 16: 14

The brain

The brain would be a channel of communication of the form of the thoughts and a battery of their insistence on the body and the outside world where they could then become effective directly, communicating themselves without physical means from mind to mind, producing with a similar directness effects on the thoughts, actions and lives of others or even upon material things.

Sri Aurobindo, 16: 37

The heart

The heart would equally be a direct communicant and medium of interchange for the feelings and emotions thrown outward upon the world by the forces of the psychic centre. Heart would reply directly to heart, the life-force come to the help of other lives and answer their call in spite of strangeness and distance, many beings without any external communication thrill with the message and meet in the secret light from one divine centre.

Sri Aurobindo, 16: 37

The will

The will might control the organs that deal with food, safeguard automatically the health, eliminate greed and desire, substitute subtler processes or draw in strength and substance from the universal life-force so that the body could maintain for a long time its own strength and substance without loss or waste, remaining thus with no need of sustenance by material aliments, and yet continue a strenuous action with no fatigue or pause for sleep or repose.

Sri Aurobindo, 16: 37

The soul's will

The soul's will or the mind's could act from higher sources upon the sex-centre and the sex organs so as to check firmly or even banish the grosser sexual impulse or stimulus and instead of serving an animal excitation or crude drive or desire turn their use to the storing, production and direction towards brain and heart and life-force of the essential energy, *ojas,* of which this region is the factory so as to support the works of the mind and soul and spirit and the higher life-powers and limit the expenditure of the energy on lower things.

Sri Aurobindo, 16: 37-38

Subtle organs

This might go so far that these organs might cease to be indispensable and even be felt as too obstructive: the central force might use them less and less and finally throw aside their use altogether.... The central force might substitute for them subtle organs of a very different character or, if anything material was needed, instruments that would be forms of dynamism or plastic transmitters rather than what we know as organs.

Sri Aurobindo, 16: 38

A mightier race

A mightier race shall inhabit the mortal's world.
On Nature's luminous tops, on the Spirit's ground,
The superman shall reign as king of life,
Make earth almost the mate and peer of heaven
And lead towards God and truth man's ignorant earth
And lift towards godhead his mortality.

Sri Aurobindo, 29: 706-07

Awakening divinity

A heavenlier passion shall upheave men's lives,
Their mind shall share in the ineffable gleam,
Their heart shall feel the ecstasy and the fire,
Earth's bodies shall be conscious of a soul;
Mortality's bond-slaves shall unloose their bonds,
Mere men into spiritual beings grow
And see awake the dumb divinity.

Sri Aurobindo, 29: 710

Bodies of immortality

These separate selves the Spirit's oneness feel,
These senses of heavenly sense grow capable,
The flesh and nerves of a strange ethereal joy
And mortal bodies of immortality.

Sri Aurobindo, 29: 710

A divine force in tissue and cell

A divine force shall flow through tissue and cell
And take the charge of breath and speech and act
And all the thoughts shall be a glow of suns
And every feeling a celestial thrill.

Sri Aurobindo, 29: 710

Matter shall reveal the Spirit's face

> The Spirit shall look out through Matter's gaze
> And Matter shall reveal the Spirit's face.
>
> *Sri Aurobindo, 29: 709*

Agony shall change to ecstasy

> Thy spirit's strength shall make thee one with God,
> Thy agony shall change to ecstasy, …
>
> *Sri Aurobindo, 29: 454*

This state can now be realised

At present this state can be realised on earth by those who have prepared themselves to receive the supramental force which is manifesting. And in that state, in that state of consciousness, the body can benefit from a much better condition than the one it was in before. It can be put into direct contact with the essential truth of its being, to the extent that, *spontaneously*, at every moment it knows instinctively, or intuitively, what is to be done and that it can do it.

As I say, this state can now be realised by all those who take the trouble of preparing themselves to receive the supramental force, to assimilate it and obey it.

The Mother, 9: 110

Not subject to the law of aging

> Sweet Mother,
> What do You mean by "to change the form of that body
> at will"? For example, will a hundred-year old man be
> able to renew his body and become a young man of
> twenty-five?

Those who have a supramentalised body will not be
subject to the law of aging; consequently the question
of age will not arise for them.

The Mother, 16: 324

Athirst for that Light

There comes a moment when the body itself finds
that there is *nothing in the world* which is so worth living
for as this transformation; that there is nothing which
can have as great an interest as this passionate interest
of transformation. It is as though all the cells of the body
were athirst for that Light which wants to manifest; they
cry out for it, they find an intense joy in it and are *sure*
of the Victory.

The Mother, 9: 191

The ideal we must keep before us

But when it [*integral transformation*] is accomplished,
when the consciousness has become a supramental consciousness, then action will no longer be determined at

every moment by a mental choice or be dependent on the physical capacity: the entire body will spontaneously, integrally, be the perfect expression of the inner truth.

This is the ideal we must keep before us, for the realisation of which we must strive; but we must not delude ourselves and think that it can be a rapid transformation, miraculous, immediate, marvelous, without effort and without labour.

The Mother, 9: 110-11

Traveller

He travels on through waking and through sleep.
A power is on him from her occult force
That ties him to his own creation's fate,
And never can the mighty Traveller rest
And never can the mystic voyage cease
Till the nescient dusk is lifted from man's soul
And the morns of God have overtaken his night.

Sri Aurobindo, 28: 72

All Nature dumbly calls to her alone
To heal with her feet the aching throb of life.

Sri Aurobindo, 28: 314